M O R E
SERMONS
T H A T
WORK

PRIZE WINNING SERMONS 1992

WITH ADDRESSES AND SERMONS FROM
A CONFERENCE FOR PREACHERS

FORWARD MOVEMENT PUBLICATIONS
CINCINNATI

Contents

ADDRESSES AT THE PREACHING EXCELLENCE CONFERENCE 1992

Preface

The contents of this volume are presented in the conviction that both the preaching and hearing of the Word of God are important and essential in the life of the church. It is the preached word which proclaims the good news of the gospel. It is the heard word which empowers God's people to discover and act on that gospel.

The first ten sermons in the book are the winners in the 1992 Best Sermon Competition. Each year the senior wardens of all the Episcopal Churches in the United States are given an opportunity to submit a sermon, preached by one of the clergy in their church, which they deem to have been especially helpful and effective. The sermons are judged by the members of the board of the Episcopal Evangelism Foundation, Inc. Cash prizes are awarded to the preachers and churches for the top five sermons. This publication gives the ten winning sermons a deserved wider readership.

The Foundation's other ministry is an Annual Preaching Excellence Program in which 45 of the most promising future preachers of the Episcopal Church gather for an intense week of work on preaching ministry. Five conferences have been held, the most recent in June, 1992, at the College of Preachers in Washington, D.C. The ten staff sermons were "homilies to future preachers" and were delivered to the conference community during our regular worship services. We feel that the quality of these sermons is such that they too should reach a wider audience.

Two other important addresses complete this book. Both were delivered at the Preaching Excellence Program as well. The first is by William Willimon, Professor of Christian Ministry and Dean of the Chapel at Duke University. This nationally famous preacher from the Methodist tradition speaks powerfully to the issues and opportunities for preaching in an Episcopal setting, or what he chooses to call "the Thinking Person's Church." The second address is by Mrs. Pam Chinnis, the first woman to be elected President of the House of Deputies of the Episcopal Church. Mrs. Chinnis gave the seminarians her view of the church in the years immediately ahead.

The Best Sermon Competition would not exist save for the generosity of John C. Whitehead of New York City. Thanks must also be extended to the Board of the Episcopal Evangelism Foundation and its President, Dr. A. Gary Shilling whose contributions and efforts are indispensable in our ministries.

Our works are only made possible by the gifts of those who see the value of what we do. Tax deductible gifts may be sent to The Episcopal Evangelism Foundation, 1335 Asylum Avenue, Hartford, CT 06105-2295.

(The Rev.) Roger Alling, Jr.
President, The Episcopal Evangelism Foundation, Inc.

PRIZE WINNING SERMONS

First Prize

Servant Woman

I would speak this morning for our children baptized this day. I would speak this morning for those who are dead and speak no longer. I would speak this morning for those silenced by a history that pretends that they never spoke at all. I would speak for those who have no voice to speak for them on this earth. I would speak this morning for a woman.

A woman who was a member of this church. A woman who was, we may surmise, baptized in this congregation. A woman who lived into adulthood in this congregation. A woman buried from this church in the year 1859. A woman whose very identity is shrouded in mystery, for the records of deaths in this parish for 1859 simply identify her as Servant Woman.

I want to speak for Servant Woman this morning. And for Servant Woman I would offer this text from Revelation 20:

And I saw the dead, great and small, standing before the throne, and the books were opened. Also another book was opened, which is the book of life. (20:12)

For years I've wondered what that Book of Life really is all about. I've known that in some sense that book represents the spiritual listing of the saints, so to speak. But on a deeper level of both meaning and reality, I wondered just what this Book of Life really is all about.

I found my answer in Malachi 3 where the prophet Malachi says:

Then those who feared the Lord spoke with one another; the Lord heeded and heard them, and a book of remembrance was written before him of those who feared the Lord and thought on his name. "They shall be mine, says the Lord of hosts, my special possession on the day when I act, and I will spare them as a man spares his son who serves him." (3:16-17)

When I saw that, I realized that the Book of Remembrance spoken of here by Malachi is really a way of talking about the memory of God. That's what the book was that Moses talked about in Exodus 32. That's what David was talking about in Psalm 69; what Daniel spoke about in Daniel 12; what Jesus talked about in Luke 10; what John talked about in Revelation 20. The Book of Life is the *memory of God!*

To be remembered by God is to be drawn into the nearness of God's embrace and Presence. To be in the nearness of God's embrace and presence is to be in heaven. The Book of Life is a way of talking about heaven. It's a way of talking about God's kingdom. It's a way of talking about paradise; It's a way of talking about "over yonder." It's a way of talking about that "great gettin' up morning," Canaan Land, the Promised Land, Beulah Land, that land over Jordan. It's a way of talking about being within the embrace of God's memory so that you don't suffer any more; you don't hunger anymore; you don't weep anymore. The former things have passed away. That which is broken is mended. That which is partial is made whole. That which is incomplete is completed. That which is wounded is healed. That which is wrong is righted. The Book of Life is a way of talking about the memory of God. It's a way of talking about heaven.

As I looked at that list of our beloved dead, I noticed that before the end of the civil war, there are numerous entries without specification, without an actual name.

You'll see "child," "stranger woman," "old man," "servant woman," "slave man," "slave woman," "slave girl," and on and on and on. Our records begin with 1859. We no longer have the records for the years between 1824 and 1859. But we may safely assume that the records of those years contain similar unspecified entries.

We know the reason for this. This church, then named Saint James' First African Protestant Episcopal Church, was a congregation of African people in America, some slave and some free. And it should therefore be no surprise to us that our records contain a significant number of unspecified and unnamed people. Slaves often didn't have names.

We need to understand that slavery was a human holocaust designed to destroy the humanity of the African in order to create a cheap source of labor. During the indignity of chattel slavery in this country slaves were therefore stripped of their very names. Their tribal and ancestral identities were destroyed. Their humanity was obliterated, at least as far as their masters were concerned. And obliteration was the point. The point was to destroy their humanity and thereby create a slave. It was a holocaust.

So their names were taken away from them. To assume some means of identification they either adopted the plantation name or just made up a name. Stop and think for a moment. Do you really think my name is Curry? Curry is Irish. Do I look like I'm from Ireland to you? Curry is not my real name. And most of your names are not your true ancestral names either.

We need to understand that slavery was a holocaust of unimaginable proportions designed to destroy the humanity of your ancestors in order to create a slave. How many millions died in those awful sardine hulls of slave ships in the Middle Passage? How many died in futile attempts to escape? How many died from diseases in the

11

New World? How many died within as families were broken, as children were separated from the parents, as husbands and wives were parted forever? How many died, feeling "like a motherless child, a long, long way from home?"

No they didn't have any real names. Their names were destroyed in the holocaust. Their identities were obliterated in the order of things. Oh, if you are as fortunate as an Alex Haley, you might luck up and trace your ancestry back to the Motherland, but that is very rare. For most of us, family genealogies won't go too much past the Civil War because our families were literally destroyed in the Holocaust. There is no name. The name is lost. That's why Jesus meant so much to our folk. Didn't they sing: "I told Jesus, be all right, and He changed my name. I told Jesus, be all right, and He changed my name. I told Jesus, be all right, be all right, be all right. I told Jesus, be all right, and he changed my name." Servant Woman.

I've been thinking about her a lot. I wonder who she really was. Was she one of those tough sisters? Was she real little, nice and quiet? Was she big, loud and bombastic? Was she evil and cantankerous? Was she a complex mixture of all of the above? Did she have children? Does she have descendants? Who were her parents? Who was her momma? Who was her daddy? Where did she come from and where did she go? Who are you Servant Woman? Something about you causes deep wondering in me. I want to know who you are. You haunt me like a phantasm from my past. Oh, sometimes it causes me to tremble, tremble, tremble.

I'm trembling because I know who Servant Woman is. I know here. I know exactly who she is. She's my great, great, great, great grandmother. She's your great, great, great, great grandmother. She's a grandma.

She's one of those "black and unknown bards" that the poet talked about. She's one of those unknown nameless folk of every race and every color and in every generation who are forgotten by this sinful and wicked world. She's grandma, forgotten by this world but remembered by God. Servant Woman.

Let every child baptized this day know and never forget that you are a proud and honorable descendant of Servant Woman. Let every child in this church rise to the greatness of your God-given destiny. You do not descend from nothing. You are a grandchild of Servant Woman. And it is your bounden duty to rise up and attain what she was never allowed to even contemplate. You must complete her destiny in your life. So rise up. Claim your high calling. "Let Ethiopia hasten to stretch forth her hand unto God." Rise up Ethiopia; you are a descendant of Servant Woman. Let us never forget her.

So what shall we do with her? Shall we weep for her? Maybe. Should we mourn her passing? I suspect they did that in this church in 1859. Maybe we should really just ignore her. No! Maybe we should get angry that a system would do this. Maybe we should start hating some folks. No, we are Christian. So what should we do? How should we react?

What shall we do with Servant Woman? More to the point, what shall we do with death? It's death I'm talking about now. What shall we do. For the issue in Servant Woman's death is really the issue of death.

When I die you can build a mausoleum and write: "Here lies Michael B. Curry, beloved Husband, Father, Pastor and Friend. May He rest in peace." All of that I hope will be true when you write it. I hope you won't have to lie. But even if you do it won't matter what you write because the winds of time will eventually erase everything that you have written about me. I will eventually wither and decay from memory and all earthly reality. Some day someone will come along and wonder who is buried under that gravestone. They might decide that since nobody knows who's buried there they might as well build the new highway over it all. In other words, the world is going to eventually forget all about you and me. What happened to Servant Woman will eventually happen to us because that's what death means—obliteration, destruction, termination! So when I ask what shall we do with Servant Woman I'm really asking what shall we do about our deaths. We are Servant Woman. Servant Woman is us. "It's me, It's me, It's me, Oh Lord, standing in the need of prayer."

So what shall we do about Servant Woman? I would submit that we don't have to do anything for Servant Woman. We don't have to do anything because there is a Book of Life wherein all is recorded and nothing is forgotten. We don't have to do anything because there is a Book of Life which is the memory of God. The winds of time cannot take that away. The verities of history cannot take that away. What God has written God has written. What God remembers God never forgets.

Don't worry about Servant Woman. She's all right. Don't you remember the thief on the cross with Jesus? All he had to do was pray, "Jesus, remember me when you come into your kingdom." His only need was to be remembered by God. "Today, thou shalt be with me in paradise." So don't worry about Servant Woman. Just pray. She's all right. She's all right. She's in the Book of Life. She's in the memory of God. And what God remembers he never forgets.

"Do Lord, O do Lord, do remember me. When I am in trouble, do remember me. When my cross is heavy, do remember me. When I'm weak and sinful, do remember me. When I don't know what to do, do remember me. When my tears are all that I see, do remember me. When the world has forgotten all about me, do remember me."

God of our weary years,
God of our silent tears,

Thou who hast brought us thus far on our way;
Thou who hast by thy might,
led us into the light;
keep us forever in the path, we pray.
Lest our feet stray from the places, our God, where
we met thee;
lest, our hearts drunk with the wine of the world, we
forget thee;
shadowed beneath thy hand may we forever stand,
*true to our God, true to our native land.**

Servant Woman? Servant Woman? Can you hear me?
I love you, grandma!

Michael B. Curry
St. James' Church
Lafayette Square
Baltimore, Maryland
All Saints' Sunday, 1991

*James Weldon Johnson, "The Negro National Anthem"

The Glory Gift

Several years ago at our annual vestry retreat, I showed a short film to begin our time together. It was a documentary about Maestro Zubin Mehta conducting the Los Angeles Philharmonic Orchestra in a performance of Ravel's "Bolero." There was nothing in the movie about Christianity or church. Yet we found it to be a profoundly religious statement, and one with valuable insights for church members to discover. The film began with scenes of the orchestra unpacking on the concert stage; men with rolling racks set out chairs; other people lugged in boxes of scores and jumbles of music stands. Timpani came out of their traveling cases, and tubas were assembled. There was the busy sound of people who knew their business getting ready to do something important. Then there were scenes of individual musicians, still in street clothes, an elderly french horn player, a young cellist, and interviews with some of them talking about their lives as musicians, about the music of Ravel, about their part in the score. Finally, an interview with Maestro Mehta, who spoke of rehearsal schedules and the pacing of the music. In all of it there was a mounting sense of anticipation.

The next scenes from pre-concert rehearsals communicated Mehta's personal intensity. He was calling each player for the best individual effort and providing the leadership by which all of it could be combined into the unified sound which is what "symphony" means. And then they played the "Bolero." I don't know how well you like this sort of romantic piece, but I find it delightful. I remember the Spoleto finale under the stars of a June night some years ago, when we stretched on blankets by

Middleton's lakes and heard the Spoleto orchestra's performance of "Bolero." If you know this music, you remember that the piece builds from a bassoon solo to a great crescendo with clashing cymbals and the whole orchestra forte, and with the last notes, the Spoleto fireworks began, and it was glorious!

Glorious—that's a word some of us used to describe the film about Mehta's version of "Bolero." In its normal use "glorious" means worthy of honor and praise—not just perfunctory compliments, as in "Good job, Zubin! Nice music!," but something more. What makes anything worthy of honor and praise is the degree to which it reflects what is ultimately true. Glorious symphony music hints at an underlying order in creation that is painfully absent in most of life. We live in discord and our own self-serving instincts contribute to the cacophony of the human struggle. You know what I mean. Relationships between people bring hurt as well as joy and will not work without sacrifice and struggle. Gardens planted to delight the eye or fill the larder will be consumed with weeds or worms unless we bend and sweat to stay ahead of the earth's corruption. Because we struggle against so much that is out of order, we like to be reminded that somewhere, somehow there is an order to things, an underlying harmony that we feel just often enough to recognize our conflicts as unnatural. And good music points to that original symphony of creation, an echo of Eden from before everyone began to write his own score. It is glorious precisely because it points to what is true about life and about us.

Take 75 people, a good many of them sensitive folk with the passionate temperament often found in artistic people, and focus them on a score which demands their willing submission to the composer's vision and the conductor's interpretation, and in the resulting harmony there is glory. Why do such a sacrificial thing? Why join a symphony when you could play solo saxophone on a street corner and really express your individuality? Musicians will tell you they don't do it for the money! The hours of practice, the exhausting rehearsals, the perspiring moments of performance—they pour themselves out for the sake of that glory which is truth, and in thus emptying themselves, they are filled. I call it the glory gift. When we give our energies to what is true, we find ourselves energized in a wonderful way. Give glory, and wonder of wonders! glory is given back!

Music is just one way in which this phenomenon is demonstrated. The glory gift works in every part of life. Jesus knew about it. On the night before he was to die, he had supper with his friends. And he ended the evening with a prayer that began with these words: "Father, the hour has come; glorify thy Son that the Son may glorify thee." If we think of "glorify" in its common sense of "honor me, flatter me, reward me," the Lord's petition seems presumptuous. But I think Jesus meant this: "Father, in what is about to happen, show my true nature, so I can show your true nature." Remember, glory means *"that which reflects the truth about something."* Jesus went on, "I glorified thee on earth by doing what you sent me to do; now glorify me in your own presence with the glory I shared with you before I came into the world." In other words, "God, by my loving faithfulness in human form I've shown the world your true nature. Now let me enjoy in paradise the true nature which we have always shared." The glory gift. When we devote ourselves to what is true, we are glorifying it, and by our participation in truth we are glorified!

This is the reason why that film about an orchestra was an appropriate metaphor for a Christian church. We are called together to glorify God, to recognize his true nature in Jesus, and in giving him glory, we enjoy, for a while, the experience of being our true selves. That's why worship is at the heart of what a Christian church is called to do. Many of us have heard this theme repeated often during our Week of Worship. We worship God not because his ego needs inflating, but because he truly deserves worship, and in truly offering it, we are acting out the truth about ourselves. We are dependent creatures, not masters of the universe! What a relief we can find in true worship! Coming in here from a world in which we are always struggling to manufacture and maintain an image of self-sufficiency, we can fall on our knees with a great sigh and be children.

I've seen my own daughters mostly grown up, seen them each make their way through adolescence with all its pressures to be accepted, to be very sophisticated, to create and hold in place that all-important image. Then from time to time along the way I've seen them able to relax and feel the joy of just being themselves, skipping unself-consciously along a deserted beach with a natural spontaneity that obviously felt good and was a joy for me to see. It's that way in worship. We come here to acknowledge the truth about God, and in so doing, we discover the freedom to claim the truth about ourselves. We are beloved children, free in these moments to enjoy the presence of the one who loves us without reservation. And to bask in the knowledge that our worth does not depend upon our performance. We say, "God, you are worthy of glory and praise." And he says, "My beloved, so are you!" We say, "But what about our sins?" And he says, "I have taken care of them, and I want you to believe that you do not glorify me when you disparage yourselves! You are my children, and you are equipped for wonderful, challenging things!" It's the glory gift. Glorifying God glorifies us. Recognizing his true nature teaches us the truth about ourselves and sets us free!

A Christian gathering for worship is like a symphony performance. First, it's a corporate venture. Someone might be able to play the violin beautifully and derive a certain amount of pleasure from drawing good sounds from the instrument, but it's not the same as making music with an orchestra. Solo performance reflects the harmony of creation less perfectly than symphony. This is God's invitation to those Christians who say, "I worship God on my own. I don't need to go to church." Not only are you depriving yourself of the glory gift, but our sound is diminished, our ensemble is flawed because of your empty chair in the orchestra. Good people need each other's music!

Secondly, diversity is celebrated! Seventy-six trombones would make an impressive noise in a big parade, but in one famous marching band, it took 110 cornets right behind to make real music. The richness of the symphony comes from the marvelous blend of strings and brass and reeds and percussion. And the richness of Christian worship depends on a similar blending of all sorts and conditions of people—men, women, young, old, parishioner, visitor, Republican, Democrat, blue collar, professional. The more diverse the congregation, the more the Maker of all of us is glorified, and the more his glory gift is felt. Because it's harder for us to play our part in concert with others who are obviously different. So when it happens, glory! God save us from the bland liturgical sterility of people who are like exactly the same kind of music and from the liturgical arrogance of people who insist that only their kind of worship is appropriate.

As in a symphony, our own worship is corporate, our diversity is celebrated, and a third similarity is this: our praise must be practiced. No good musician would expect to let his instrument sit in its case all week long and then hope to produce satisfying results when concert time rolls around. But too many church folk let their devotional lives go flat Monday through Saturday and come to church on Sunday unprepared to offer anything for God's glory. Worship is what we come to give to God. The glory gift begins with the practice of his presence day by day so that on Sunday we can say with personal assurance, "God is good!" And as we pour ourselves out, singing enthusiastically, responding clearly and audibly, listening attentively, we'll be wearied in worship as a symphony player is poured out in performance, but wonderfully filled. Sunday worship requires practice all week long.

Here's a fourth similarity: as in many great orchestral scores, Christian worship calls for variations on a single theme; a symphony which introduces new musical ideas each moment may be technically challenging and artistically impressive, but what delights audiences, and I think satisfies musicians, is that moment when a single theme can once again be recognized. Now the woodwinds have it, now the strings. It's what stays in the memory and defines the piece of music. It's the same with Christian worship: we have a wonderfully rich musical heritage—from the ethereal sound of a monastic choir to the spirited hymns of a Gullah praise house.

Among the Baptists and Lutherans and Roman Catholics and Pentecostals and Episcopalians, the unifying theme is *Jesus*. In his prayer, Jesus said to his heavenly Father, "I'm praying for those you have given me. *I am glorified in them.*" What the Father invites us to do is glorify Jesus. He has sent the Holy Spirit to make this happen. It's no good to sniff, "I don't buy all this 'Jesus' business. I've come here to worship *God!*" If you understand anything about the God of heaven and earth described in Holy Scripture, you'll realize that he's focused all of himself in his Son. You do not honor God when you by-pass Jesus. He is our focus by God's explicit plan, our constant unifying theme by which the Father is glorified.

Finally, the church at worship is like a symphony in performance in its need for direction. Somebody must wield the baton, set the pace, announce the entrances,

21

ask for volume, balance the sections. That is the clergy's job, for better or worse. Conducting worship, like directing a symphony, requires the priest to have an intimate knowledge of the composer's music, and a trusting relationship with the musicians. What makes a symphony a reflection of eternal harmony is the remarkable willingness of skilled musicians to discipline themselves for the common good. It won't work to have the bass section insisting on one tempo while the percussion people want to go faster; neither is it helpful for the strings to insist on rehearsals at one time while the woodwinds would rather practice at another. Sometimes the music calls for one section to carry the theme, other times the musicians are asked to sit quietly and rest, following the score while others play. The glory of God is his loving nature. When we glorify him, that nature begins to be reflected in us. We learn patience and gentleness and self control.

In the film on "Bolero," conductor Zubin Mehta is seen as a constant encourager of his musicians! Hearing a particularly happy piece of music, he shouts to that section, "You are wonderful! Magnificent!" Hearing a flaw in timing, he corrects with a firm authority that might be felt as arrogance by those who hadn't gotten to know him. "No!" he says, "Too fast! We must build together!" A good conductor is challenged in leading an orchestra of 100 professionals. A leader of worship conducts the efforts of volunteers — 30 or 300 — he never knows 'til they show up.

But together, by the mercy of God, we give and receive the glory gift. When we tell God what we think of him, he tells us what he thinks of us. We might never play in a symphony and feel the exhausting exhilaration of concert performance, but we can look forward to an even richer blessing, right here, or wherever we worship God, week by week, in a symphony of praise. Jesus said, "Father, glorify thy Son, that the Son may glorify thee." And so we pray, "Lord, you have glorified us in Jesus; now we are here to glorify you, to recognize and celebrate the truth about you, how you have shown yourself faithful through generations, and loving even when we fall; we glorify you for who you are. Now, Lord, glorify us again, fill us again with your version of what we're worth, that we might show a fragmented, self-seeking world what it's like when sisters and brothers are together in supernatural harmony. Accept from us, poor players all, the glory gift, and make of us virtuosos of praise, in an endless symphony of worship. Amen."

Richard I. H. Belsar
St. Michael's Church
Charleston, South Carolina
Easter VII, 1990

The Last Word Is Always Victory

Funeral of Linda Sue Windel Brown

2 Samuel 12:13-14; Psalms 91 and 139; Ephesians 4:29—5:4; John 17:20-26

The lessons which Linda chose for this occasion speak of her powerful experience of faith. They begin with a story that portrays the sorry outcome when human inclinations to live in ways not pleasing to God prevail. David has been adulterous, and even though honest and repentant and forgiven, he finds there will be consequences. Because of his earlier scorn of the Lord, the child to be born of the adulterous union will die.

From this somber text, the lessons moved to Paul's Letter to the Ephesians in which a list appeared of other behaviors equally dangerous to the human enterprise: bitterness, wrath, anger, wrangling, slander, malice, lust, greed, bad language. With a list like that we should all be shaking in our shoes. Alongside this suggestive though hardly exhaustive inventory of human sin, is the simply stated alternative of being imitators of God who live in relationships expressive of the love Christ has for us, love marked by kindness, tenderheartedness, forgiveness.

And finally we heard in the Gospel the portion of Jesus' so-called "high priestly prayer" in which he prays that all who believe may be so steeped in the goodness of divine love that they will in turn become expressions of it that draw others into its fold. A summary statement which pulls the connecting pieces of the three readings into a theme goes something like this: life presents seemingly irresistible temptations whose consequences are dire; the antidote to falling prey to them rests in the love of God which offers satisfaction far more fulfilling than any other source; and when this love is accepted as the shaping dynamic of one's life, it can turn the recipient into living, breathing testimony to the incomparable joy of life lived in faith—living, breathing testimony to the incomparable joy of life lived in faith.

Does that sound like anyone you know—living, breathing testimony to the incomparable joy of life lived in faith? Of the many phrases used to describe Linda that I have heard in the last few days, none has been more oft repeated than her irrepressible joy, her unswerving optimism, her capacity to make every circumstance, no matter how complicated, untoward, grievous, even seemingly impossible, into an occasion fraught with hope, new life, opportunity, victory.

A sixth-grade student fortunate enough to have had Linda as a resource teacher quite some time ago reported yesterday to Judy Muntner, principal at Damascus Elementary where Linda last taught, remembering how even when everyone else had become exhausted trying to help, "Mrs. Brown knew what to do. She believed in us and could always find a way to help us learn whatever we needed to master." Teachers echoed the sentiment, reporting that when their frustration had reached its limit, Linda was a "no-problem, can-do" helper who found a way to solve the issue.

A friend from Community Bible Study remembered how concerned Linda was several years ago, when there was just a daytime group in Damascus, about people who could only come at night. Linda began a satellite evening group which quickly grew to twenty, then thirty participants and now numbers upwards of seventy-five meeting every Monday night. Nothing was a problem for Linda; what most would consider a perplexing dilemma or even an outright catastrophe, Linda viewed as an exhilarating challenge. When *we'd* be praying prayers for help or deliverance, *she'd* be offering up thanks for another opportunity to experience and draw upon the power of God.

Her encounter with multiple myeloma was no different. In the letter she and Clint wrote on June 5, 1989, to inform their friends of this new episode in their lives, they described their reaction as one of "excited expectation." That is a quote, dear friends gathered here, that is a quote. "Excited expectation" is how they responded to this invasion of cancer into their lives. They believed that what the medical world describes as blood cancer which is progressive and life-shortening was an opportunity to grow and to witness to God's power and love. Lest you read into these words a pie-in-the-sky kind of cheeriness or a naive attempt to put a gloss on a desperately sad reality, I hasten to assure you that they wrote also of crying a lot, and of hearts breaking to think of the prospect of dreams not completed and of their love for one another interrupted by death.

But these tears and anguish poured forth from inner lives whose most vital parts were not the sinew and muscle and organs and bone we think of, but the love of God which knew them and indwelt them and called them by name before they were knit together in their mothers' wombs.

Linda wrote in her 1980 journal (twelve years ago!) these words: "At the center of my life is Jesus Christ. My body is the flesh that clothes his presence." Her life goals from that day on—again recorded in her journal—were to nurture this center of her being so that as wife and mother and family member and friend she would reflect this love of God made known in Christ, and as human being she would live in such ways as to point others, whom she came to know, to its very Source. Is it any wonder such a woman would choose lessons that together declare the love of God to be both the hope of the world and the joy of life? With the understanding of that divine indwelling love to be her true inner essence, and of her flesh simply to be the garment which clothed it, she knew that what was real about her, what was at her core, was not assailable, even by such a dread disease as multiple myeloma.

The *hope* was that the power of that divine presence would radiate from that precious center within her, and from the similar center of others who shared her faith, and bring physical healing into her flesh, and oh how we gave ourselves to that end in prayer and song and sacrament. And lest we despair that all this outpouring of holy energy was apparently fruitless, let me remind you that it is not results which validate faith, but faith which sustains, no matter what the results.

And the faith was that physical healing or not, the encounter with this cancer was providing ongoing and ever deepening ways to glorify God and make known the incomparable joy of life surrendered to divine care. And it was, of course, this latter which finally became the reality that has brought us here this night. Physical recovery did not take place. Her flesh gave out. But the inner life it clothed only grew stronger and more vibrant and finally broke loose and went to her heavenly home, as the garment which was her body weakened and broke and bled and finally breathed its last.

And if her life goals included (which they did) inspiring in her family and close friends the grace of faith she knew so intimately, then she died with this fondest wish granted. For grace was abounding in that room on eighty-ten Seneca View Drive in the final watch of what had become a vigil whose outcome everyone there knew. It came in her husband's tender words of love and assurance, his minute by minute, hour by hour, ministrations of touch and prayer and water and word. It came in

Christy's steady presence and ready surrender of her mother to God Almighty, all the while brushing her hair to help her as she struggled to make the transition from here to eternity. It came in Jeremy's indomitable spirit of hope which, as he came in and went out of that room, made him know that there was a gradual getting better going on there far more profound than physical recovery. It came in her mother's and father's and sister's meticulous attentions to her aching bones and cold feet and parched mouth and bleeding nose and in their unceasing efforts to make her comfortable. It came in the steadfast caring presence of her foster son, Brian, and of her dearest and best friend, Karen, whose faithfulness tended to Linda's every final need as she gradually let go on the final day of her life. It came in the flood of caring and concern expressed in the prayers and calls and visits of friends and family, young and old, from near and far, that punctuated that day.

And if her life goals included (which they did) pointing others to the source in whom she lived and moved and had her being, your presence here today makes me believe that God's welcoming words to her as she slipped through heaven's gates were, "Well done, thou good and faithful servant."

There are dangers here, however, as there always are in the experience of a faith like Linda's, and one is to think that its blessings are restricted to the especially courageous or pious or chosen or outgoing or smart or gifted or particularly suited. But that of course would be to distort disastrously the grace of God which takes unlikely folks like Sarah, frightened ones like Moses, unsuspecting ones like Gideon, flagrantly sinful ones like David, pagan ones like Cyrus, reserved ones like Mary, simple ones like shepherds, inept ones like Peter, and turns them into witnesses for God. Faith is never an accomplishment of which to boast; it is rather a gift for which to offer thanks.

And the love which generates such a gift is poured out on you and on me no less than on Linda.

Another danger is to think, "Wait a minute. If this God Linda was so surrendered to and found such joy in did not spare her the agonies we know she suffered, what good is faith?" The error in such thinking is to construe faith as some kind of magic that—if we'll just do it right—can ward off the terrible things life seems quite regularly to bring. The truth is that faith rather rarely changes circumstances, but always changes us, and we, in turn, can change at least some of those circumstances and when we can't, it is by faith that we can live and die through them like Paul the apostle, and his sister in faith, Linda: afflicted, but not crushed; perplexed, but not driven to despair; persecuted, but not forsaken; struck down, but not destroyed; mortally wounded, yet alive with joy.

And there is yet one more danger that I shall speak of before drawing this sermon to a close—the fear that, despite faith, suffering and death in the end really do have the last word. Linda died and we hurt. If our stories of faith contained only the kind I have alluded to thus far, we would have cause, at this point, to throw up our hands in defeat. But from Ezekiel's testimony about the valley of dry bones into whom the Spirit of God breathed life and breath, to that of the apostles and the women who found the garden tomb empty, to that of contemporary witnesses like Linda, people of faith have always known the power of God to be resurrection power. And in that stunning good news comes the comfort and consolation that death is never the end for those who have crossed its threshold, nor is grief the final lot of those who mourn their passing. For God who gives us life, gives it to us again and again and again, promising that smiles will return to the faces of those who mourn on this side, and that fulfillment, with all the saints and angels, awaits those who have made the journey to the other. And so the last

29

word, my friends, is always victory—dry bones breathe, Christ is risen, grace abounds, the Spirit moves, God is with us, here and in the hereafter, now and forever more. Alleluia. Amen.

Karen B. Johnson
St. Anne's Church
Damascus, Maryland
January 15, 1992

Aids and the Disciplined Life

Out of the sports page and onto the front page of the major newspapers, the magic of Ervin Johnson grabbed the attention of the world two weeks ago. As popular an athlete as there has ever been, Magic set a world in dialogue over one of the big issues of the nineties, "safe sex" and the promiscuity that requires it.

The attack on the immune system which we call AIDS is no longer a disease of a homosexual or needle-using population. It knows no sexual preference and it is no longer gender-selective or restrictive. You have probably seen the widely publicized statistics that now demonstrate that the fastest growing population on a percentage basis is women.

This issue is not easy to address from the pulpit, not predominantly because of the sensitive nature of the disease, but because of the complexity of the issue. I would like to address this often mutilated subject from a Christian perspective.

First of all, groups concerned with AIDS and many churches across the land have shown and are showing their compassion for the victims of the virus. As in all periods of history, the church is at its best when it reaches out to the sick and those who hurt, whether or not the hurt or sickness is of their own fault. Compassion is the highest virtue for any Christian. Before anything else we define ourselves by our willingness to reach out to those in need. Jesus' words ring through the ages into this age. "When did we see thee sick and visit thee? Inasmuch as you have done it unto one of the least of these ye have done it to me." Christianity is a religion which breathes life and hope into its adherents when those who believe minister to those in trouble, sickness or distress. And so it is quite right and imperative for our mission group, for our parish, for our congregation in worship to spend our energies on behalf of those suffering.

But, there is another side to this issue which is harder to address. What does the Christian church have to say to a world which has liberated itself from monogamous sexual behavior? Since AIDS is primarily a sexually transmitted disease, it has gotten our attention in a way that the Bible and Christian tradition have failed to do over the past few generations.

I remember reading the book *African Genesis* by Robert Ardery. One of the main themes of the book is that two instincts are left in human nature. One, not surprisingly, is *survival*. The other is that human beings, for about as long as they have been human beings, have been *making better weapons*. The author argues that this latter trait is so strong it is on the level of a human instinct. The two primordial desires, the need to survive and the need to make better weapons, once on the same team, so to speak, are now on a collision course. Which will win out is the big question? Will our need to survive out-duel our need to dominate by virtue of a better weapon? The question still looms, but perhaps arms control is the first tentative answer to this question.

In this issue of transmitted sexual disease, particularly among the young people of high school, college age and beyond, there is a collision course apparent between the seemingly cultural right to sexual relations with several partners perhaps over many years and a disease which is devastating and directly proportional in risk to the number of sexual partners one has. The cultural pressure born of decades of stimulation from media of all kinds has created nearly a sacred bill of sexual rights, and now it butts against a threat which does not come from ethical persuasiveness, but directly from the same biology which produces human beings in the first place. Which perspective will win out? I confess that the majority of the male population of a few years ago was rather quick to say that this must be God's punishment of the gay and drug-using community. That was a somewhat comfortable position for many. Locker rooms filled with middle-aged males were more than open about that sentiment. But, it was only a matter of time before the limitations of that perspective became apparent. The handwriting is on the wall. Regardless of its origins, AIDS is a disease of promiscuity, of needles, or of sex.

Denial of this reality is rampant. Dear and very lovable Magic Johnson, I fear, has not yet gotten the best message. I hope he does a lot of good—he has a magnificent platform and he is obviously courageous and charismatic enough to influence many. But, I hope he learns to espouse a different message. Safe sex is also a trap. Safe sex is perhaps eighty-five percent safe. That is a heck of a game of Russian roulette. Even the message of safer sex which at least defines the situation more accurately does not reach the center of the problem.

Unless a cure is found for AIDS, humanity, and particularly our children, will lose this game of roulette. When I last spoke of AIDS from the pulpit it had not yet reached the college community. It now has. The possibilities are frightening. Across the country there are now apparently two million Americans who carry the virus. That is one in a hundred people, but unless behavior changes radically the disease will win. Behavior is changing among a small group of the population at risk, but among the majority safer sex is still the leading motto. Abstinence and faithfulness are still a very silent minority.

Sex among the young or uncommitted is primarily a

matter of hormones, not a matter of love. The love words are usually used in order to mask the truth, but love is not usually at issue. The truth as *desire* is dominant and *discipline* is recessive, but the love vocabulary makes it sound better.

We are entering a new age when true love must battle for supremacy—love of family, love of God, love of real relationship, love of discipleship—for the other is the love of illusion, the love of escape and the love of self. Usually the latter, love of all those illusions, requires the denial of God. The needle and promiscuous sex have a lot in common. They both are caused by a loneliness which requires a fix. They both are unsatisfied with the momentary pleasure. They each have to keep finding a partner who will help them escape the pain they feel, and because relationship is not the goal, they fail again and again.

Much of society finds escape in substituting this and that for relationship, for God, but few substitutes for real relationship are as devastating in effect as this disease. The root cause of all this is denial of our primary purpose and denial of who we are and to whom we belong.

Will it be AIDS that drives us to our knees? It is to You, Oh Lord God, that we belong. It is to You that we come for primary sustenance. It is loving our neighbors as ourselves that connects us in real and lasting ways. It is to real love that we must give ourselves—body, mind and spirit. Nothing less will save us. Is that an exaggeration or is that the truth? We Christians must decide.

Let us pray.

Stephen D. Parker
St. Matthew's Church
Wilton, Connecticut
November 24, 1991

Where's John the Baptist?

Mark 1:1-8

It's time for Christmas shopping. Yes, I know — this is Advent, a time when the church reminds us to wait patiently for the coming of Christ. But in the world Christmas is coming, and you and I have Christmas presents to buy. So tonight we're going to go Christmas shopping — and this is going to be major shopping, because we're going to the mall.

Imagine driving to the mall, parking your car, turning out the lights, pulling the keys out of the ignition. It's so dark the lights over the vast parking lot barely shine through the thick fog. You step out of your car, and the air is so cold, the damp so penetrating, that the ice is already forming on your windshield. You shove your hands into your pockets and walk as fast as you can to the doors of the mall.

Now this is no ordinary shopping mall; it's a brand new suburban mall. You enter it through glass double doors, and all of a sudden you've left the dark, and the damp, and the cold behind. Everything inside is brand new, shining with chrome and glass, and the air is warm; it's at least 70 degrees in here. You walk into the main part of the mall, and everywhere there are bright lights — Christmas lights and colors shining on the glass and the chrome — and everywhere there are people talking, hurrying, shopping.

For those shoppers who get worn out by their hunting and their hurry, there are places to sit down and rest, benches surrounded by bright green artificial grass, and in the very center of the benches there's even a fountain.

This mall is the equivalent of the old village square. It's the place where people not only go to shop; they go to see and be seen. And this is the mall at Christmas time, so there are even more people tonight in the shopping parade. As we walk, Christmas carols come to us over the sound system, and everywhere there are packages—in the windows, on the benches, in the arms of people shopping. Mothers and fathers, grandmothers and grandfathers are holding the hands of small children, patiently waiting to see Santa Claus. Packs of teenagers are walking up and down the mall—boys walking down this side, girls on the other side, eyeing each other while they shop.

Every shop window, it seems, has a creche in it. There are elaborate Italian creches, silver and gold and crystal creches, ceramic creches and hand-carved wooden creches. And in every creche, in every window, we see the people of the Bible story—the shepherds and their sheep, the wise men and their camels, the angels and cherubs, Mary and Joseph, and even baby Jesus. It's all so lovely . . . but: where's John the Baptist?

The church's Advent lessons mention John over and over again, but we never see him! Week after week we hear about John in the lessons, but we never see him in the Christmas windows, we never see John in the mall.

Now imagine this: in comes John, right into the mall. It's deep winter, but he's wearing sandals on his bare feet, and, yes, he's wearing his camel's hair coat, tied with a leather girdle. Now he strides through the double doors of the mall and comes out into the open space near the fountain, and he's crying out, "Repent!"

Unreal! What's this awful man got to do with Christmas? Get him out of here, so we can get our shopping done!

But wait; imagine this: John is a powerful preacher,

and the adults cease their frantic shopping and start to gather round him. The teens stop their wandering to laugh, but then they find themselves listening. The children hear him and leave Santa's line, tugging on their parents' coats and asking questions:

"What's he doing?"

"What's he saying?"

"Why is he here?"

What's John saying? He's crying out: "Repent! turn around! change your lives!" And John is such a powerful preacher that the lights, the carols, the creches, the shopping, the seeing, even Santa's line — all are forgotten, and people begin to ask, "What shall we do?"

And John says, "Repent, and be baptized."

Then he begins to baptize them, right in the beautiful mall fountain. Young men and boys stop worrying about what their friends will think, and go right into the waters with John. Teenage girls take off their leather boots before they step into the waters. Mothers and grandmothers leave their packages on the benches, and walk into the waters. The shopkeepers come out of their stores, and go into the waters with John. And John keeps pushing them under the waters, and baptizing them through and through.

Now what does this baptism for repentance mean?

John says, "Turn around, and change. Be baptized to signify your willingness to change. Then be willing to have your lives changed from the inside out."

John says, "If you are shopping for clothes, don't buy another coat; if you have two coats, share with someone who has none."

John says, "If you are planning a holiday meal, don't spend more money on elaborate food; if you already have food, share with someone who has little."

John says, "If you are a merchant, don't cheat your

customers; give them honest bargains. Deal with integrity."

John says, "Repent! Change your ways! Turn around, and face reality!"

And what is reality?

According to John, this is what is real: not the shopping mall, not the glittering lights, not the presents and packages, not the Christmas carols, not even the lovely creches which remind us of the coming Jesus. Reality is the cold and the dark and the struggles of the world outside, and reality is the One who is coming, the One who comes to warm us, who comes to give us light, who comes to comfort us in our pain, who comes to strengthen us in our struggles.

John says there is One coming who is real, One who can help us live with reality—One who can give us life.

So, what shall we do with John the Baptist? Shall we keep him out—push him out of the mall—so we can hear the carols instead of his voice?

Or shall we let him in, allow him to speak, to preach in the mall, so we can open our ears and hear the Word?

John says there is One who comes in the power of the Spirit, whose Light can open our eyes to see, whose Word can open our ears to truth, whose Spirit can give us life—power to live with our eyes open, power to live in the world outside the mall.

What shall we do with John the Baptist this Christmas?

Donna Ross
Christ Church
Oberlin, Ohio
Advent II, 1991

Misplaced Anger

Mark 13:14-23; Hebrews 10:31-39

We all can probably remember a child from our school days who was the class scapegoat. This was the unpopular child who was slightly different in some way from the rest, and for this reason, was singled out by the class. We can imagine today as adults how painful the experience of scapegoat was for the lost child of our school days. The scars caused by blame and scapegoating may not always be physical, but they are psychological and they run deep into the soul.

We are aware of what happens when repressed anger and frustration from the workplace finds its expression in the home. In the extreme, it results in child or spousal abuse. In the main, it exists in bitter arguments over finances. The expectation today is that anger is not to be expressed in the workplace or at social occasions. When this anger is not expressed in the appropriate places, it seeks expression elsewhere, often at an abstract target, a symbolic authority figure or a scapegoat target that is not likely to return the aggression.

Most often, we are mystified by the emotion of anger, often unaware of the engines which drive it, and the source of our true frustrations. Anger is then dumped on a likely target. However, I would like to suggest that much of popular anger is misplaced. Instead of finding expression where it might produce some constructive change, it is so often unleashed in a destructive fashion, at those unpopular targets called scapegoats who probably won't fight back.

Such was the case in the 1930s, when the world economy found itself in deep depression after a crash on Wall Street in 1929. Many thousands of people were poor, hungry, and deprived of the promise of material fulfillment. There was the easy dichotomy dividing all human beings into one of two categories: the rich and the poor. On this apocalyptic landscape of pent-up frustration in post-World War I Germany, Jews faced a desolating sacrilege unlike any other in history, before or since. It began with an unlikely leader, an obscure demagogue, who had served as a corporal in the army during the war. He was a paper-hanger by trade. And this obscure demagogue used an evil genius to play upon the pent-up anger and frustration of the German people, and he turned that anger on the Jews. By making use of popular prejudices, he propelled himself into power.

In Daniel's day, the demagogue's name was Antiochus Epiphanes. In St. Mark's day, he was likely known by the name Nero. The names of these demagogues live on in infamy in every generation down to our own. They were the desolating sacrilege which threatened to destroy justice and goodness in the world.

Last week, while I was visiting Dr. Nelson Burr, we spoke of his days in the Library of Congress in Washington, D.C. In the 1950s, Dr. Burr was in the midst of his career in Washington. I asked him what those days were like when another demagogue succeeded in capturing the angst of the populace: Joseph McCarthy. Nelson characterized his actions as a form of "psychological terrorism" which led nearly everyone in Washington to live in fear. Dr. Burr pointed out that McCarthy even attacked the Library as misleading the Congress with Communist intentions.

And just this week, another demagogue of our time, David Duke, former leader of the Ku Klux Klan and a Nazi, almost led a successful campaign for the statehouse in

Louisiana. It is interesting to note how he denied that the holocaust ever happened in Germany. Two weeks ago, after other Hartford area religious leaders and I spoke out against the present violence associated with the tax debate, another demagogue, active right here in Connecticut, said he was skeptical that any violence has occurred, and that at the very least, it has been exaggerated by state legislators, according to a Hartford Courant story.

Today in Connecticut we stand at a moment with striking similarities to the past. We live in an apocalyptic landscape with many frustrations and disappointments: a failed economy, lack of job security, layoffs, a deep recession and a serious diminishment of our hopes, dreams and aspirations, especially the material ones. The frustration is widespread and it runs very deep.

We are also at a crossroads when expectations about the "American Dream" are being forced to change. As the number of people who join the world economy multiply each day, in Eastern Europe and what was once the Soviet Union, the pie in whose bounty we have all shared isn't getting any larger. It simply means we will have to share a little smaller piece if everyone is to be served. These are people with the same hopes and dreams and aspirations as we have. However, if their standard of living is to rise about the pitiful conditions in which they exist, it means our standard of living must change to make room. Such change means there will be many who will be very frustrated. In Connecticut, I would suggest, we have begun to engage this change in the standard of living head-on. For the average middle-class household, the income tax was the straw that broke the camel's back and awakened these growing frustrations.

Into this apocalyptic landscape come the false prophets who as Mark suggests will seek to lead astray the elect. They are the demagogues, the modern abomination of desolation. These are they who tear down, attack and destroy for their own self-aggrandizement, finding the opportunity ripe for their own demagoguery.

I am not here today to advocate or oppose the state income tax. That is the job of the state legislature. However, my responsibility as a Christian and a pastor is to stand up for justice, fairness and civility. As Christians, we are taught to uphold and respect the dignity of every human being. We are taught to stand against violence and hatred, those abominations which today threaten the desolation of our land.

Let us turn for a moment to what I call the litany of shame. Some of the violence is physical. Some of it is psychological and emotional. It is not unlike the psychological terrorism of which Dr. Burr spoke. Consider and remember, please, in this context, when our governor was spat upon, not unlike our Lord's treatment on the road to Calvary, or the state legislator's wife whose car was run off the road because it bore the special marker plates, or when a state legislator's home was victimized by a drive-by shooting. Remember the threats against State Representative Miles Rappaport (a well known Jewish leader), at which time he was also the victim of a hateful religious and ethnic slur, being told to "return to Russia." The latest incidents in this sad litany include those surrounding the "Legislator du jour" campaign. It would have been appropriate if letters of concern were solicited. It would even be appropriate to encourage the public to call their legislators at the office. However, the systematic campaign of harassment by passing out home phone numbers has solicited, among legitimate calls, numbers of threatening, obscene and psychologically terrorizing calls to the children and spouses of legislators. This is wrong, and to it we must say a loud, NO!

Why should Christians be concerned? Why speak of it to a congregation on Sunday morning whose members are not likely to be participants in such behavior? It is because when such behavior exists, good people must stand up and be counted on the side of justice, fairness and civility. Few stood up to speak out against the demagogue in Germany in the 1930s. Most feared retribution in speaking out against the demagoguery of the McCarthy era in this country not so long ago. We know that Jesus would stand against violence and with its victims. We must now line up and stand on those lines also.

In the Book of Hebrews this morning, the author recalled the "hard struggle with sufferings and sometimes being publicly exposed to abuse and affliction, and sometimes being partners with those so treated." Christians and Jews know firsthand what the author of Hebrews means. I can speak from personal experience also, having had my home phone number posted on the public airwaves in similar fashion when I spoke out last year about the "Steve and Tramp" doll which made fun of the homeless. Today, I stand with those who are victims of this violence, this emotional terrorism, and I stand with you as your partner. You are not alone. I call upon all people of good intention in our state to join me in being partners against such violence and intimidation!

We have had enough of the "me generation" and the "me, my, mine" attitude. It is time for another attitude to prevail. It is time to be a "We people" again, like the first words of our constitution suggest: "We the People." It doesn't say, "Me the people." Christians are a "we" people, and today we stand up to say, "We care!" AMEN!

Chris Rose
Grace Church
Hartford, Connecticut
November 17, 1991

The Price and the Promise of Evangelism

Will you proclaim by word and example the Good News of God in Christ?
I will, with God's help.
(Book of Common Prayer, p. 305)

The Book of Common Prayer identifies four occasions in the year when "Holy Baptism is especially appropriate": the Easter Vigil, the Day of Pentecost, All Saints' Day (or the Sunday which immediately follows), and the Feast of the Baptism of our Lord (that is, the First Sunday after the Epiphany). And there is one other particularly appropriate occasion: the Bishop's visitation, since the Bishop is the principal minister of the Sacrament of Baptism throughout the diocese. And these five times are meant to be so closely associated in our minds with Baptism that, even if there are no candidates to be baptized on any one of these occasions, we are still urged to renew our baptismal vows that day. To renew them as a reminder of all that God has done for us and of all that we have promised to do in response with God's help.

But this morning there is a candidate here to be baptized, and there are others who have come to confirm the promises made for them when they were too young to answer for themselves, and there is one person whom we shall receive and welcome as a new member of the worldwide Anglican Communion. And in preparation for their Baptism or Confirmation or Reception we shall together be renewing our own Baptismal Covenant. With that in mind, I want to speak about one of the questions

I shall put to all of you as part of that Covenant, and the answer you will give to my question:

Will you proclaim by word and example the Good News of God in Christ?

I will, with God's help.

As many of you know, the various Provinces of the Anglican Communion and many other Christian bodies throughout the world have designated the closing years of this century as a Decade of Evangelism. This ten-year period leading up to a new century, indeed to a new millennium, will begin three weeks from now, on Advent Sunday, December 2. That gives special urgency to my question to you and your answering of it. And all of this has a special appropriateness under this particular roof, because St. Andrew's is named for the first Christian missionary and evangelist, and because your rector, Erik Larsen, and his family have just gone to proclaim the Good News of God in Christ in another part of the Anglican Communion. For him, and for Karen, and for each of us in this Decade of Evangelism, what is at stake is our faithful response to the Great Commission given us by our Lord:

Jesus came and said to them . . . "You, then, are to go and make disciples of all the nations . . . and, remember, I am with you always, even to the end of the world."

(Matthew 28:18-20)

These words of Jesus remind us that all evangelism has a price attached to it, and a promise. First, the price: "You, then, are to go and make disciples of all the nations." And secondly, the promise. "And, remember, I am with you always, to the end of the world." That promise alone makes it possible for us to pay the inevitable price of evangelism. The price of breaking ties and building bridges for the sake of the multitudes who (in the words of one of our prayer book collects) "have been created in [God's] image but have not known the redeeming work of our Savior Jesus Christ" (Book of Common Prayer, page 257, prayer 16). The price paid by every generation of our forebears in the faith.

On June 9, when the bell summoned the community to midnight prayers, they found the old abbot in front of the altar. He lay there dead, a smile on his face, surrounded now for the last time by his companions, those with whom he had established the great monastery of Iona. Ever since that June day in the year 597, St. Columba has been commemorated as a "pilgrim for Christ."

Almost a thousand years later, again as it happens on June 9, the first Book of Common Prayer came into use throughout the Church of England. Listen to Dom Gregory Dix's memorable words: "With an inexcusable suddenness, between a Saturday night and a Monday morning at Pentecost 1549, the English liturgical tradition of nearly a thousand years was altogether overturned" (*The Shape of the Liturgy,* p. 686). The events of that June day can also be commemorated as we turn the pages not of the first but of the ninth Book of Common Prayer this morning.

Now when it comes to evangelism, you and I can hardly be accused of acting "with inexcusable suddenness"! The Episcopal Church, in all truth, is more like the tortoise than the hare, though, of course, we can take encouragement from the final outcome of that fable! Yet, as soon as we take evangelism seriously, we shall find that it entails for us what it entailed for St. Columba and for our sixteenth-century Anglican ancestors. It will mean, without any doubt, some breaking of ties, some building of bridges.

Columba's biographer tells how, at the age of 42, in

what today would be called "a mid-life career change," he "sailed away from Ireland to Britain, wishing to be a pilgrim for Christ." Think of what this meant for him in the way of breaking ties: ties with his family, ties with his earlier missionary endeavors, ties with his homeland. Yet he chose Iona expressly because, from its highest hill-top, the Irish coastline and all it represented for him could no longer be seen. On the Eve of Pentecost he and his friends landed on Iona and then, on Pentecost Sunday, in the power of the Spirit, they sang the Lord's song in a strange land, the land that was to become their home. And for the next thirty-four years Columba evangelized the Scottish mainland, proclaiming by word and example the Good News of God in Christ. And when Columba died, it was the year 597, the very same year in which, by the wonderful providence of God, St. Augustine arrived far to the south in Canterbury to become eventually the first "Archbishop of the English Nation."

And the same costly breaking of ties was involved in the introduction of the first Book of Common Prayer— and, as we know so well, the introduction of every subsequent prayer book! Ordinary folk found English substituted overnight for Latin, active participation in the liturgy demanded in place of private devotions, treasured customs laid aside in favor of new practices, and the sacrifice of the Mass replaced by the bread and wine of the Lord's Table. Understandably, they ached for the old and the familiar with the same yearning that drew Columba's thoughts back again and again to Ireland.

Yet, however much he longed for Ireland, Columba spent the rest of his life building bridges between the gospel of Jesus Christ and the multitudes he encountered in the course of his ministry. Tirelessly he preached and taught, healed the sick, comforted the sorrowful, and counseled the troubled. The penitent, the poor and the perplexed were alike his concern. And by his prayers and labors, and those of his companions, countless folk, created in God's image, were brought for the first time to know and worship God as he has been revealed to us in his Son.

Centuries later, Thomas Cranmer and his fellow bishops were bridge-builders, too. As a new social order emerged around them, they wanted to relate the gospel of Jesus Christ to the ordinary folk of their day. The 1549 prayer book, in the language of the people, had a stated goal shared by every prayer book since: ". . .That the people . . . should continually profit more and more in the knowledge of God, and be the more inflamed with the love of his true religion" (*1979 Book of Common Prayer,* p. 866). Cranmer meant it to be what it and all its successors have become: a bridge between Christian faith and human experience, between the promises of the gospel and the hopes of human hearts, between daily liturgy and daily life.

And Columba's experience and Cranmer's experience will be ours as well in the course of this Decade of Evangelism. Each of us in this and every other congregation will be called to pay the price of evangelism. We will be asked by God to let go of those private agendas and even of that intimate fellowship which congregations establish for themselves and cling to tenaciously. Old and familiar ways of worship, and times of gathering, and forms of ministry, and standards of individual giving and of clergy remuneration will be questioned as to their appropriateness and effectiveness as we reach out to win back the lapsed and to evangelize the unconverted.

And even the strong, silent types among us (the classic Episcopalians!) will learn, slowly and painfully perhaps, to speak of what God has done in their lives and longs to do in the lives of those among whom we live and work. For in the coming Decade of Evangelism the responsibility of speaking God's word and of bringing God's healing touch to bear on so many different lives and situations will rest squarely on your shoulders as much as on mine, or Father Ken's, or Father Erik's far away in Hong Kong. For that is the sure consequence of living out our baptismal promise to proclaim by word and example the Good News of God in Christ.

Yet this breaking of ties, with all the learning and growing and changing that will be involved, will be for the sake of building bridges. Jesus' Great Commission to make disciples of all nations will mean—indeed, does mean in some place already—Spanish prayer books in Anglo pews; Haitian and Filipino and Korean congregations under Episcopal church roofs; Afro-American spirituals and Hispanic songs in Episcopal hymnals; and children of all shapes and sizes and noise-levels in once solemn assemblies.

Bridge-building of this kind is often resisted because it is certainly discomforting for us and certainly a departure from the old and the familiar. But recall that the ultimate bridge-building was done for us all in the form of the cross. And that cross was willingly taken up and carried by one who broke all those ties which would have held him back from fulfilling God's Great Commission. The commission to proclaim the gospel to people everywhere, the commission he now invites us to share with him.

And in inviting us to share in the work of evangelism, Jesus does for us what we must also seek to do for each other. He identifies, affirms, equips and supports each one of his followers, filling us with the grace and power of the Holy Spirit. For only the Holy Spirit can give us the faith and courage we need to break the ties of class and family, education and race, accepted church custom, and personal preference and ambition. Only the Holy Spirit can give us the love and patience we need to build bridges between the community which is nourished by font and

49

pulpit and altar and the hungry, confused and divided multitudes who as yet know not our Lord. Only the Holy Spirit can enable us to open the doors of our hearts and the doors of our homes and the doors of our churches to strangers. Only the Holy Spirit can empower us to find the words and live the lives required of us in the Decade of Evangelism. Only the Holy Spirit can help the candidates and their families and each one of us to keep the promises we are about to renew this morning, including our solemn commitment to proclaim by word and example the Good News of God in Christ. Only the Holy Spirit, who was at work in Jesus and is now at work in the world and in the church and in each one of us, can do all of this.

And that is why the promise contained in Jesus' Great Commission matters so profoundly, for that promise of his makes it possible and indeed desirable to pay the price involved in all true evangelism. For when Jesus says to us, "You, then, are to go and make disciples of all the nations," he also assures us, "Remember, I am with you always, to the end of the world." And because we know from experience how true those words of his are, we can make our promises confidently this morning. We can do so, believing that all things are indeed possible "with God's help." And for that we can give thanks, even in a time of international tension and national uncertainty, even in a time of transition and change for our diocese and for this congregation of St. Andrew's in Marbledale.

Will you proclaim by word and example the Good News of God in Christ?

We will, with God's help.

Jeffery Rowthorn
Bishop Suffragan of Connecticut
St. Andrew's Church
Marbledale, Connecticut
November 11, 1990

The Story Behind the Story

The Feast of Epiphany, which we celebrate at Heavenly Rest this morning, has become for many a kind of second Christmas, nearly as dramatic and evocative as the first. A miraculous and peripatetic star appears in the sky over Palestine, prompting three kings to descend their thrones and leave their far-off lands and search together for the newborn king of the Jews. The sinister King Herod reluctantly assists them by directing them to Bethlehem, where they find the child with his parents, pay their respects, and offer him precious gifts. They evade Herod on their way home, intuiting that he is up to no good. Good triumphs over evil: the holy child has been found and recognized and given homage by the world.

This story lives in us in a very deep place. But I suggest to you that it is not because it records a simple triumph or because it is either romantic or probable, at least not in the way we have ordinarily appropriated it. Recent scholarship suggests that the three men who followed the star to find Jesus were not kings, or philosophers, or even astronomers. They were more likely astrologers, or even magicians, dabblers in the divination of the supposed influence of the stars and planets on earthly affairs—the New Agers of the first century, so to speak. In the religious world of that time, astrological speculation about the date of the Messiah's birth was common, just as speculation about the date of the end of the world is today. So it looks like the three wise men weren't royalty, but marginal religious practitioners like those found in any age. Add to this the fact that the story does not have a happy ending.

If you read a bit beyond today's Gospel reading, you see that the three searchers were correct in suspecting that Herod had something up his sleeve. Because of his encounter with them, Herod too was able to locate Jesus, causing the holy family to flee for their lives to Egypt. As a result of what we celebrate on Epiphany, therefore, Jesus was made a refugee. All of this changes our picture of Epiphany, of the journey of the three magi, but let's lay that aside for a few moments.

The reason this story speaks to us so directly, I think, is because of what it tells us about power and our various encounters with it as we make these less-than-royal journeys that are our lives. Power is a pretty loaded topic these days, one about which we receive many messages. The Christian church tells us that as people of faith we ought not to be concerned with power, that the spiritual life consists of surrendering power and aligning oneself with the powerless. On the other hand, our therapeutic culture encourages us to nurture our personal sense of empowerment, to take control of our lives, to refuse to be a victim. Wherever we find ourselves on this spectrum, my sense is that most of us remain profoundly ambivalent about power, with our actual experience of it seemingly elusive. Today's Gospel helps us locate the powers in our lives, it helps us reflect on their intents, and it helps us name the places to which our decisions about them lead us like a star.

Consider two powerful characters in the story of the Epiphany. First, Herod. He was the puppet king who ruled the Jewish people in Palestine from 37 B.C. until a few years after Jesus' birth. He was a crafty militarist and political maneuverer who was smart enough to marry a woman who was a member of the Jewish royal line, thereby giving himself a touch of credibility with his subjects. Famous for his cruelty and paranoia, he wanted no threats. He had his own sons murdered when he thought they stood in his way. Herod knew what he wanted, and he always got it. Ironically, he was known as "Herod the Great."

When the three magi arrive on his doorstep and tell him that they have knowledge that a new king, the real king of the Jews, has been born—and right under his nose—he panics. He finds out from religious Jews where scripture has predicted that the Messiah will be born, and he tries to trick the wise men into revealing the whereabouts of the child. When they elude him, he takes the blanket approach to eliminating any threat to his power. In a fury, he massacres every male child in the region of Bethlehem who is about Jesus' age.

Here's what's important to remember about Herod: that he's not an aberration or an exaggeration. For the most part, the world works as Herod works—by force. By the world, I mean it as the Gospel of John means it: the drug lords, slum lords, war lords, money lords, as well as our more personal dark lords of pettiness, envy, lust, and the rest of those two-bit mobsters of the soul—all the powers that deal death, that say "no" to life. The world rejects God and fears God and like Herod does not want him found. In order to insure that God and his truth are not found, the lords of this world can and do resort to anything to keep falsehood on its throne. They will trick, they will deceive, they will collude, they will create refugees, they will even murder their own children and massacre others. They will nurture a culture of cheap sex and cheap drugs and cheap guns and genteel neglect that ensure that those who have escaped the massacre will live stunted lives. They will panic at the very mention of truth, however small, however gentle, however inviting. Like Herod, the princes of this world fly into a rage when their power is threatened, and because their power is maintained only by the threat of violence, they must use violence to preserve it. The powers that be know exactly what they want, and they take it—generally behind a smoke screen of righteous rhetoric.

The second powerful character, Joseph. Now Joseph is far quieter than Herod. In fact, he is completely invisible in this story. We never hear him say a word, ever. There is not one word of Joseph's recorded in the whole New Testament. Yet his role in the story of the Epiphany is pivotal.

Joseph is one of the good guys, "a just man" the Bible calls him. We first meet him when he is engaged to Mary, a young woman also well-known for her piety and goodness. Yet things go wrong for them from the start. Mary is discovered to be pregnant—by whom, no one seems to know, and Mary's explanation is enough to make all doubt her sanity as well as her piety. Joseph is willing to break the engagement quietly to minimize the scandal, and though we can admire his discretion we can also imagine his suffering. His dreams for the future lost, his wife-to-be unfaithful before the fact, so to speak. He certainly looked to have been played for the fool; even he must have found Mary's story hard to believe. And yet one wonders whether behind his disappointment, beyond his inevitable sense of betrayal and confusion and embarrassment, was not anger, not panic and rage, but a rather different emotion.

An angel gives a hint of it when he appears to Joseph in a dream. The angel tells him, "Joseph, do not fear to take Mary as your wife, for that which is conceived in her is of the Holy Spirit." Joseph, do not fear to take Mary as your wife. The fact is, Joseph still wanted Mary. He longed for her. The angel encourages him not to succumb to convention, but rather to take what he wants—although not in the way of the world.

Joseph will marry his beloved, but he will be an altogether different husband to her than he had thought he would be. They would have a child, as they undoubtedly had hoped, but it will be a different child than they had imagined. In seeming contradiction of the entire structure of reality, never mind the movements of the sun, the moon, the planets, and the stars, Joseph will become the father of a son who is not even his. The angel asks Joseph to tear himself away from the life he wanted, and thought he was headed for, in order to make something else possible.

Which, of course, is the finding of God and his worship. Because Joseph gave up the power to control his life, Jesus entered this world according to God's plan. Because Joseph let his plans get lost, the three wise men were able to find the Lord of life. Three grown men kneel before God—that's why this story sends its roots deep down in us, because it reminds us of what we are made for, of what we really want, the worship and love and praise of God. Once we have given up our claim to the power to run from that all our lives—the power of money and sex and drugs and success and intelligence and favor and fame and the most subtle power of them all, the power of convention, the power of the way the princes of this world tells us that things should and must be—once we have given up all that, nothing can keep us from what we are made for.

How do we begin to find Him? How do we begin to search? How do we begin to be that community of searchers we call the church?

Perhaps a first step is in admitting that, like those high-class palm readers we have made into wise men and kings, we are not quite what we have cracked ourselves up to be. What a relief that is, to admit that no matter how hard we try we can't put our lives together perfectly, that no matter how craftily we try to figure out everything under the sun so we can have it all under our thumb, we will sometimes get lost, we will always need to stop and ask for directions, we will not at every turn be sure of where we're going, we will always be, like the wise men, in some sense at the mercy of others. We will always need each other on the way.

Then, too, we need to face up to Herod. To see the array of evil forces, large and small, that drag us away from our search for God, and that will use any means necessary to do it. If you doubt there is evil in your individual life, think about the last time you manipulated a situation to get your way, or, if you're really brave, think about the last time you lied. If you doubt there is evil in our corporate existence, think about the last time you saw a human being sleeping on the floor of a subway station. And if you want to see the connection between the two, think about the lie you told yourself about why you can't do anything to help. Evil, like Herod, always tries to mislead us, to pretend it really doesn't have something up its sleeve. We need to face up to the Herods in our lives—or, perhaps, to face up to the Herod who is our life.

And then, of course, we need to be like Joseph. Here's the wonderful thing about Joseph: he was transparent to God. Wedged between the private scandal of Mary's pregnancy and the public intrigue of Herod's plots, Joseph listened to his dreams. Do that these days and you're considered certifiable. We can't follow our dreams the way we follow road maps, but remember: we've gotten so good at fending God off in our waking lives that sometimes the only way he can get through to us is by catching us unawares in our sleep! Listen to your dreams, and to every one of your unguarded moments. God is often there, leading you onward in your search for him. And like Joseph, entertain the possibility that what you really long for lies somewhat behind or beyond what it is you think you want. Consider the possibility that God has something in mind for your life that you haven't even thought of yet.

Take your search seriously. The fact that you're here

in church this morning—take that seriously. It's a miracle! That may seem an unnecessary thing to say, in this age when we all tend to take ourselves overly seriously, but most people don't take their spiritual lives nearly seriously enough. Don't minimize your sense of how God is trying to reach you. Spend some time alone, in quiet. Consider that the power you are being called to is Joseph's power, the power to know that it is possible to live without power in this world.

Lastly, don't be afraid to worship. Is that a funny thing to say to a huge group of church-goers? I don't think so. In this time of great social needs and great personal needs, every church has taken so much upon itself that we easily forget what the church exists primarily for—the worship of God. The three wise men didn't go on their journey to help other people, though eventually that may have been one consequence of what they did. They didn't go on their journey to make friends, though getting to know each other better was surely one of the "perks" of their long trip. They went in order to find God and to worship him, to kneel before him and offer him the most precious gifts they had, their lives. They saw who he really was, and recognized him as their hearts' desire. That's worship, that's the truth. And the power of that truth will not only heal our lives. It will also lead us like a star to that ultimate truth, which is that all the lords of darkness that confuse and deceive and mislead and massacre are but pretenders to the throne, their power, ultimately, only sleight of hand. The real Lord, the true power, the King who gives hope and life—he is among us already. My brothers and sisters, do not fear to take him as your heart's desire.

Anne Richards
Church of the Heavenly Rest
New York, New York
January 5, 1992

Baptized with Fire

Luke 3:15-16, 21-22

Rachel Carson opens her great book *The Sea Around Us* with this fabulous understatement: "Beginnings are apt to be shadowy." Shadowy indeed! Downright mysterious is perhaps more appropriate. In her book Carson tries to unravel some of the mysteries of the genesis of the vast oceans which surround us. And those beginnings are, for the most part, shadowy and unclear.

The beginning of the ministry of Jesus Christ is no exception. It all started at his Baptism of course, an event so strange and misty that for most of us the story requires that we suspend our rationality for a few moments. We are, after all, told that the "heavens opened up" and that a dove-like figure descended upon Jesus and a "voice came from heaven." It seems so incredible that many of us are tempted to slip past this story and get on down the street to something more concrete.

But we are not going to do that this morning. There is a symbolic core to this story, a central element seen dimly between the shadows (but necessary for all baptisms) on which element I want to focus for the next few moments. My goal is to help us understand why this moment of Jesus' baptism was so important for him and is so important for us. In fact, I'm happy to confess working with this passage has given me a fresh insight into who Jesus was and why he actually can help us.

The symbolic element of which I speak is the water of the Jordan River. It could be any river, it could be any water. What was so special about that water?

Before we look more closely at the water, however, let me remind you of something. In the Bible there are four versions of the baptism of Jesus. The stories presented by Matthew, Mark, Luke and John agree on certain particulars, but there are some tantalizing details in which their reporting differs markedly, perhaps even profoundly. For instance, Luke is the only writer who points out, quite emphatically, that Jesus was baptized *last,* after all the people had been baptized. Uncharacteristically, Jesus was not with the people when he went into the water. He was the last person baptized.

Why did Luke report it this way? Well, we have to use our imaginations a little here. No one knows for certain what went on in Luke's mind so, perhaps, your imagination is as good as mine. But why would all those people, hundreds, maybe even thousands, come to John to be baptized? It's pretty clear to me. They needed help, big time help. They were those whom society had labeled "sinners," of course, but there were others there, too, with different labels. Included in the crowd no doubt were the weak, the lame, the blind, the deaf and the sick. Some came on crutches. They were the crushed ones, the bruised of society. They were led by their friends; perhaps some came secretly. All needed help with their lives. So John baptized them in the water of the Jordan, which meant for them that their afflictions, their sins, their weaknesses were washed off into the river. And here is the central theme of my thoughts this morning. The river into which Jesus walked after all these people had been washed clean was teeming with the myriad sins and weaknesses and handicaps that had been symbolically washed off of hundreds, maybe thousands, of people—those who had been baptized before him.

So if you ever wondered why a sinless person such as Jesus needed to be baptized by John—and Christians have wondered that for centuries—here is an answer: In the waters of the Jordan River Jesus was totally immersed into sin and weakness and helplessness, the raw humanity of life. Jesus emerged from the Jordan River totally identified with all the bruised and crushed people of the world. And from that moment on he had this strange solidarity with those who were his societies' weakest folk; prostitutes, tax collectors, adulterers, people possessed by the devil, sick people, blind people, deaf people, thieves.

The point here is that Jesus characteristically reversed the expected order of things. You and I and every other human being in the world go into baptism as an unclean sinner, weak and ineffective. We come out of baptismal waters clean, forgiven and empowered to be the people of God. Jesus went into baptism clean and pure and sinless and he came out totally identified and connected to the sins and infirmities of the human race. Thirty years after his glorious birth—the birth of the Son of God—this was the moment, not that Jesus became God—he was born God's son—his baptism was the moment Jesus became truly human.

The point that Jesus' baptism makes clear is one we all know: the only way we can truly help someone is to identify and empathize as much as possible with them. By dirtying himself in the waters of baptism, Jesus took upon himself all that we are. "For our sake God made Jesus to be sin who knew no sin . . . " (2 Cor. 5:21). Indeed, "he has borne our infirmities and carried our diseases," and "the Lord has laid on him the iniquity of us all" and "by his stripes we are healed" (Isaiah 53). The question is, of course, what then might we do?

Three short vignettes might help us get closer to this event—one quite personal, one about the disease AIDS and one about the issue of homosexuality.

The personal story: A few years ago I was not at all able to help or understand people who were deaf. This despite the fact that in one of the churches I served as rector, I was directly responsible for a congregation of deaf people. They met in my parish every Sunday in the downstairs chapel; they had sign language services and were very active in the church and in the community. I was rector of that parish for six years and I never learned a word of sign and hardly paid any attention to the men, women and children who attended the deaf services. In fact, I hired someone to take care of that congregation so I wouldn't have to be bothered.

But now I have been baptized into the deaf world. I have been washed in the waters of those who cannot hear anything and I know more, so much more. Involuntarily, I have become deaf without being deaf.

An example from the AIDS crisis: A bishop whom I know leads a diocese in which there are an enormous number of people dying from AIDS, the Diocese of California. One Sunday, a few months ago, this bishop had a service of Holy Eucharist for men and women and children and their families of his diocese who had AIDS. Hundreds attended the service at the cathedral. He distributed communion bread and wine to every one who came to the altar. After the last person received, the bishop put the cup of wine to his lips and finished all the wine that was remaining. Most of us feel that is a perfectly safe act, but symbolically everyone knew what was happening. This was a baptism into the illness of AIDS.

A final example, this one dealing with the gay community. As some of you know, homosexuality is an issue that is tearing at the seams of our church today. A friend from seminary recently wrote a letter to the church suggesting that every Episcopalian, gay or not gay, should join the group called Integrity. That's the support organization within the church of Episcopalians who are gay. My friend is not gay; he is married with two children, but he has decided to voluntarily be baptized into the gay community—to help them carry the burdens of their lives—to become gay without being gay.

Maybe this is what John the Baptist meant when he said: "I baptize you with water; but one who is more powerful than I is coming; I am not worthy to untie the thong of his sandals. He will baptize you with the Holy Spirit and with fire." A lot of people are not aware that Jesus never baptized anyone with water—only with the Holy Spirit and with fire. Maybe at the baptism of Jesus we can see through the shadowy beginnings and glimpse the meaning at its core: something about what it means to be baptized with Fire. Amen.

Craig Biddle
Trinity Church
Upperville, Virginia
January 12, 1992

On the Holy Innocents

Some of the most poignant moments I have experienced in my ministry have occurred when I have been asked to bury little children. I well recall an incident a few years ago when a young couple came to me to bury their seven-month-old daughter. The child had died in her sleep for reasons no one was able to determine, including the physician who did the autopsy. The parents' grief was all the greater because of the mystery associated with the child's death. With pain and confusion in their voices, they asked me, "Why do these terrible things happen?" And, as I spoke words of comfort to them, in the privacy of my thoughts I too asked that ancient and haunting question, "Why do bad things happen to good people?" as Rabbi Harold Kushner put it in his popular book of that title.

Their child was one of the Holy Innocents and December 28th is the day in the church year when we recall them. The biblical incident on which this recollection is based was the massacre of all the baby boys under two years of age in the village of Bethlehem, described in the third lesson this morning. King Herod thought that by doing this terrible thing he could get rid of the infant Jesus who, he was told, would one day be "The King of The Jews." As you know, Joseph, warned in a dream, fled Bethlehem with Mary and the infant Jesus. When the church recalls the Holy Innocents, we recall not only those children massacred in Bethlehem but all the innocent children down through the ages who have died for whatever reason, be it murder, starvation, physical abuse, sickness or disease; or for reasons known only to God, as in the case of that seven-month-old little girl whom I buried.

There are two meanings of the word innocent. First, it means free from guilt or sin through lack of knowledge of right from wrong; that is, blameless in the sense of one who knows no better. Children up to about age four or five are believed to be innocent and blameless in this sense. A second meaning of the word innocent is not guilty. I mean, if the policeman charges you for speeding when, in fact, you were not speeding, you are innocent. Even though much suffering has occurred to innocent people in this sense of the word, it is the first meaning we are principally concerned with on a day like this—blameless in the sense of one who knows no better.

From the beginning of recorded history, people have asked, "Why do the innocent have to suffer?" and "Why do bad things happen to good people?" The most obvious answer is because of the presence in the world of villains like King Herod and all of his cruel companions down through the ages; evil men and women who kill, torture, and abuse the innocent to gain whatever twisted and perverted ends they pursue.

The clear and repeated teaching of scripture is that such villains will rot in hell throughout eternity. Jesus has some strong words about child abuse. In the gospels, after identifying little children as being foremost in the kingdom of Heaven, he told his listeners that whoever intentionally hurts such a child, it would be better for him to "have a millstone tied around his neck and be drowned in the depths of the sea." Jesus recognized in the very next verse that there will indeed be those who damage and abuse the innocents in this world, but he adds, "Woe betide the person through whom such offense comes."

Jesus and Holy Scripture are equally clear about the ultimate fate of the Holy Innocents. Jesus told us that

"They have their guardian angels in heaven who look continually on the face of my Heavenly Father" (Matthew 18:10). As surely as the villains who hurt the little ones will rot in hell, the innocents themselves will be quickly ushered into God's presence and will attend him in positions of great honor. For the blameless and the innocent are whom God honors first in his heavenly kingdom.

The evil perpetrated by villains like Herod isn't the only reason the innocent suffer. They also suffer because of the sin, carelessness, error and ignorance, the sickness and disease that is everywhere in this broken world. The innocent also suffer because of the violent eruptions in the natural order from earthquakes and floods to storms and droughts. It is when we try to figure out why some suffer and others don't that absolute answers become difficult to come by, because none of us knows the mind of God in any complete way. Let me try to explain.

The bomb that drops from the sky can't distinguish between the enemy it is aimed at and the child playing in the street. So suffering is an integral part of the violence associated with war for the guilty and innocent alike. While we cannot say why this person was killed by that bomb and the person next to him was spared, we can take up our mission to be peacemakers and try to stop mankind's warring altogether.

Similarly, the invisible virus that wounds or kills one person and spares the next cannot distinguish between a good person and a villain. Suffering is an integral part of most illness. While we cannot say why one person was assaulted by a virus and another person was spared, we can support with our time, talent, and treasure the research that will one day neutralize or eliminate that virus.

Again, a great deal of the suffering in the world can be attributed to ignorance. I once knew a poor uneducated woman who didn't know that child-bearing was related to sexual intercourse until her sixth child! All her children suffered from malnutrition and abusive treatment. While we can't do anything about such things until we hear of them, we can advance the cause of sexual education amongst the poor that might limit such suffering in the future, something that is especially important in an age of HIV/AIDS. While research and analysis, study and prayer, can help us to understand some of why one person suffers and another doesn't, in the final analysis only God knows why. But, and this is so important; we do know that suffering provides us with the opportunity to do something, to help someone else, to change our outlook, to grow in ways we otherwise might not or could not.

For example, the young couple I mentioned earlier came to see me ten months later with a new, lovely, healthy baby girl whom they wanted baptized. Although they were a young couple—she was only 23—there was a subtle difference in them from when I knew them ten months earlier. They seemed to me to be much closer to one another, wiser, more religious in orientation. Suffering provided them with an opportunity to minister to one another in new and deeper ways, to grow in ways they might not otherwise have done.

No one should ask to suffer, that would be masochism. Nor should we attribute our suffering to God, for we cannot know with certainty that he is the author of it. Rather we must learn to accept suffering as an integral part of life and as a God-given opportunity to grow in the faith. Scripture makes this point repeatedly. In Romans (5:3-4) for example, we are even encouraged to "exult in our present sufferings because we know that suffering trains us to endure and endurance brings proof that we have stood the test and this proof is the ground of hope."

Victor Frankl, the famous Viennese psychiatrist who survived the terrors of a Nazi concentration camp, argues that suffering is one of the three ways we can discover the meaning of life. In his book *Man's Search For Meaning,* he writes, "For what matters above all is the attitude we take toward suffering. . . in accepting the challenge to suffer bravely, life has meaning up to the last moment."

In this regard, the Book of Job in our Bible is very instructive. If you recall, Job was an upright, God-fearing, just man. Then misfortunes and calamity struck him, and in a short time he was reduced from a wealthy man with a large family and in good health to a poor, sickly beggar who had lost everything.

Now Job was no ordinary fellow. He didn't just ask, "Why me, God?" He argued for 28 chapters that it wasn't fair and that he had been given a raw deal. Along the way he expressed a lot of anger toward God. Meanwhile, his three friends, sarcastically called "Job-comforters," argued the other side of the matter. They said, in effect, that because this misfortune had happened, Job must have sinned or displeased God somehow, some way. So they wanted Job to repent.

One of the reasons the Book of Job is such a classic is that both of these points of view about why the innocent suffer are so familiar. Again and again, I have known people, including myself, to resort to one or the other of these arguments in an effort to understand or explain what has happened to them. Some say, "Why me?" as if to say, "It's unjust and unfair because I have tried to live a good and upright life." Others take the guilty position: "Well, I must have done something wrong or this terrible thing wouldn't have happened to me."

In light of the universality of these two responses to suffering, God's reply to Job is extremely significant. He began by taking him to task for presuming to have the answers to a question that, ultimately, only he has the answer to. Chapter 38 begins, "Then the Lord answered Job out of the whirlwind," saying,

Who is this obscuring my designs
    with empty-headed words?
Brace yourself like a fighter;
Now it is my turn to ask questions
    and yours to inform me.
Where were you when I laid the
    earth's foundations?
Tell me since you are so well informed.
Who decided the dimensions of it,
    Do you know?
Have you ever in your life
    Given orders to the morning . . .
Have you been shown the gates of death
Or met the janitors of shadow land . . .
    Tell me all about it if you have!

In the Book of Job, God goes on like this for four chapters, never answering the questions of Job or his companions, never speaking to their specific arguments, but always chiding them for presuming to know something which, in the final answer, only he knows. Eventually Job responded as only a finite human being can. He said, "I have been holding forth on matters I cannot understand, on marvels beyond me and my knowledge. . . I retract all I have said, and in dust and ashes I repent."

Ultimately, only God knows why the innocent — or the seemingly innocent — suffer. Nevertheless, our duty is clear; we are asked to trust him and follow him — especially when called upon to bear heavy burdens, when faith in God's mercy is hardest to hold onto. For it is in suffering that our faith and souls are tried and tested.

Finally, we are asked to believe that God will never put more on us than we can bear: that all things do work for the good to them that believe; that the souls of the righteous are always in his hands; and that, despite all the suffering we have to bear, life not only *can* be sweet but *is* sweet.

I close by repeating the line from Romans: "Suffering trains us to endure and endurance brings proof that we have stood the test and this proof is the ground of hope." And, remember to pray for the Holy Innocents.

Robert K. Pierce
St. Paul's Church
Smithfield, North Carolina
December 29, 1991

PREACHING
TO
PREACHERS

O. C. Edwards
Professor of Homiletics,
Seabury-Western Theological Seminary

The seventies were a great time for posters. One that you used to see had a caption that went something like this: "When you are up to your neck in alligators, it's hard to remember that your original purpose was to drain the swamp."

The meaning, of course, is obvious. Life provides so many distractions that it is very easy to lose track of what you originally set out to do. While we can all probably think of a number of situations in which that has proved to be the case, the alligators I have in mind today are those that make it easy for us to forget what our preaching is really all about.

It seems worthwhile this morning when we have a congregation largely composed of people who are just beginning their preaching ministry to point out some of the preoccupations that have caused predecessors along their path to lose their way. In order to do that, however, we must first have some idea of what the goal of preaching is. You can never know that you are lost unless you know where you were supposed to be instead of here.

I assume that the purpose of preaching is to help people not to miss out on the purpose of life. And what the purpose of life is is beautifully summed up for us in a sentence from our gospel for today. That gospel is a section of the prayer that fills the seventeenth chapter of John. This prayer marks the end of Jesus' discourse at the Last Supper that started in chapter fourteen, the discourse which seems to be John's equivalent of the "Little Apocalypse" of the synoptics in that it tells the disciples what to expect in the future.

The words from our gospel that state so clearly the

purpose of human life, the purpose that preaching is supposed to remind us of, is verse three: "And this is eternal life, that they may know you, the only true God, and Jesus Christ whom you have sent."

As you know, "Eternal Life" is the phrase the Fourth Gospel seems almost to substitute for the key theological term of the synoptics, "The kingdom of God." Thus, eternal life is the salvation proclaimed by the banners one sees held before television cameras at athletic events with the legend so cryptic for non-Christians, "John 3:16." "For God so loved the world that he gave his only son, so that everyone who believes in him may not perish, but may have eternal life."

Our verse specifies the content of the promise in John 3:16. What Christians are promised instead of perishing is that they will know the one true God and Jesus Christ whom that God sent. Eternal life is knowing God, and perishing consists of not knowing God. A way of paraphrasing our text, then, is to say that "life is about God." If you miss that, you miss the boat. Life is about God. That's what we are supposed to preach. That's the message that turns us into sentinels, lookouts, and heralds.

Life is about God. Whatever else may happen to people, whatever achievements and successes they have otherwise, if they miss this, they miss what life is all about.

Now to say that life is about God is not to become otherworldly so that, for instance, we ignore social issues. John gives no support to Karl Marx's claim that "religion is the opiate of the people." Knowing God and the Christ whom God sent is not "a pie in the sky when you die by-and-by." To begin with, for John eternal life is not a place you go to after death, but begins whenever one accepts the Christian proclamation. And one's acceptance is spelled out in terms of behavior. One of John's ways of talking about the Christian life is to call it "doing the truth." And bottom line of it all for him is loving one another.

So this seeing the purpose of life to be knowing God is not otherworldliness. It simply means that if one is to live effectively in the universe one must be in harmony with the Creator of the universe and the purposes of that Creator. So life is about God. "This is eternal life, that they may know you, the only true God, and Jesus Christ whom you have sent." That's what we are supposed to preach. Seeing that people know that is the swamp we are supposed to drain.

But what are the alligators that so distract us? The first is the most basic, and that is the temptation to stop preaching to make God known and to begin to preach to advertise ourselves. That sounds pretty crass, doesn't it? So crass that it seems like something that nice people like us could never be guilty of. But let's stop to remember a few things. Let's remember back to preaching class and how we wanted our sermons to be evaluated in comparison to those of our classmates. And let's remember what it felt like when we learned that we had been chosen to attend the "Preaching Excellence Conference." Was our reaction to say, "How wonderful that I can learn how to proclaim Christ more effectively," or was it to say, "It couldn't happen to a nicer person"?

To extend this tale of woe, let me admit that staff members for this conference are not without questions about how their sermons will be received in comparison to those of colleagues. And, finally, let us admit that in the future when we know that in our congregation there will be representatives of the call committee of what our Methodists friends call "a wider field of service," few of us will be so lofty as to have no other desire than that the committee members leave our church closer to God.

So, you see, it's really fairly easy to forget to preach Christ in our anxiety to preach ourselves.

A second alligator that can prove distracting from our swamp draining is the temptation to regard the institutional prosperity of the church to be what our preaching is supposed to effect. Again, we would never state it to ourselves so baldly, but that is what much preaching is addressed toward. For instance, in the Decade of Evangelism in which the Episcopal Church and the Anglican Communion are supposed to be involved, concern about loss of numbers — not to mention loss of revenue — seems to dominate many discussions. Not those of our national commission, but certainly those of many other groups. And it's sometimes hard to distinguish between stewardship and "paying the preacher." That's not what Roger teaches as a diocesan stewardship officer, but it is what some people teach. It is said that no one was able to write a convincing biography of the Duke of Wellington until some historian discovered his checkbook. Analyzing the checkbooks of parishes, dioceses, and national church bodies might also be a fair way of discovering how badly we have been bitten by the distracting alligator of institutional success.

The third of the alligators in which we are up to our necks is becoming so involved in preaching some good cause that we make it an end in itself and not a means to an end — so that it no longer is a way of expressing our knowledge of God and the Christ God sent but has become the whole shooting match, all that we are interested in doing. I don't have to list such good causes. You know the list and may even have your pet cause that threatens to become your alternative to the gospel. Needless to say, this is the sort of temptation that only comes to good people. But that only proves the truth of the words T.S. Eliot put into the mouth of Thomas à Becket: "The last temptation is the greatest treason: to do the right deed for the wrong reason."

One last point and we are through. A major reason

why it is so easy for the alligators to distract us is that swamp draining is a muddier purpose than it seems. Knowing God and knowing Christ seem clear enough goals, but it is hard for the preacher to supply very specific content to them. Thus, for instance, in this sermon that was supposed to be about the danger of preaching that is not centered upon proclaiming that life is about God, the time has been given to warning of alternatives to be avoided rather than to saying what that knowledge is and what makes it so desirable.

The alligators bite again. So far the score is alligators four and preachers nothing. But next time maybe we can devote our attention instead to saying:

Taste and see that the Lord is Good. Happy are they who trust in the Lord.

Erica B. Wood
President, The College of Preachers

Hearing this Gospel (John 17:11b-19) and several of the "Farewell" texts again this year, I realized in the hearing that my perspective had made several seminal shifts.

In the past I always had identified with the disciples who in hearing the mysteriously proleptic words of Jesus and in anticipating his departure, must have felt frightened, confused, anxious—abandoned. The disciples at this point in the Gospel are characterized as befuddled and fumbling, overwhelmed by sadness, not even having the gumption to ask Jesus: "Where are you going?" They are childlike and in the most passive, pluperfect sense of the verb, they had been left.

But reading and hearing this Gospel passage again this year, I found myself drawn not so much to the disciples who will be left, but rather to the one who will be doing the leaving. Who knows when these kinds of shifts in perspective take place, but I suspect this one began for me sometime in the process of becoming a parent.

If I entered the delivery room, as I suspect I did, with some fair part of myself feeling like an abandoned child, I re-emerged, infant sucking at my breast, feeling like a mother bear. Suddenly the verb tense had shifted from passive to active—I was the protector, not the protected, the lover not caring about being loved, the parent, no longer the child. Somewhere in that great chamber of mystery, my capacity to love had expanded to dimensions as disproportionately dilated as the birth canal during labor and inexplicably, not even consciously, I was ready to lose my life for another.

Another shift in perspective, or at least an expansion of the first shift, was how exactly and painfully Jesus realized the eccentric and exposed position that the disciples would be in following his death. For years they had been with him, believed in him and now were like him. He was not of the world and no longer were they. He was hated by the world and the world would certainly hate them. He had fought with evil and their remaining lives would be an unrelenting struggle. No wonder he prayed fervently to the Father to give them both the power and the glory that had been given to him. No wonder, in Luke, he told them to stay in the city until they were clothed with power from on high.

It is the generative impulse of love that runs deep that makes us strive, above all, to protect our children, however they are ours. And, when we know we are leaving— whether it's our infant child with a babysitter for the evening or, certainly, the anticipation of our own death— our need to protect the ones who will be left grows more urgent and projects into the future.

I remember a house tour my mother gave me just before she died. Room by room, closet by closet, she insisted on going over each and every item with careful instructions about how to use it, where to store it, how it (whatever it was) would help me, clothe me, warm me— protect me, someday. Each item she pulled out of a drawer, unravelled from faded tissue, rediscovered in a shoebox, each item, I thought, was agony. Looking at her industry, feeling her urgency, knowing that in months she would be gone forever, it was all I could do to stay in her presence and to follow her, room to room.

But she seemed to draw energy from it. For someone who could barely breathe she tirelessly moved through the silverware, the sheets, the summer bedspreads, the summer rugs, the photographs, her jewelry, her mother's jewelry—a ring that was to go to a grandchild, should there ever be one.

It was all that she had. And, more than that, it was all

that she could do. It was her loving and brilliant plan for my protection, each item had a place and was an instrument to somehow connect us, even through death.

In the Gospel that we have just heard, what Jesus is about to leave the disciples is an invisible inheritance of protection, power and promise. His plan for their protection was no less than to transfer his own sanctification, his joy, his power to them.

Jesus' prayer to God the Father is to sanctify them in the Name of God, the Name that had been given to him. Now the disciples might be guarded, held and sanctified by the same holy Name.

His promise for their protection is that the Counselor, the Holy Spirit, will be sent to remind them of all that he has said to them, to teach them all things.

The power that the disciples inherit is no less than the love that the Father has given the Son and is what the Son now bequeaths to the disciples—"that they may be one, Father, even as we are one . . . so that the world may know that . . . you have loved them, even as you have loved me."

By our Baptism, we have inherited nothing less than the same urgent and loving plan for protection that the disciples received from the Son of God.

Room by room all that is in the Father's house is now ours through him. As time goes on, and as our perspectives continue to shift, as we prepare to be the one who does the leaving, it may comfort us to remember in our urgency and love, that the very same baptismal inheritance belongs to our children as well.

Judith McDaniel
Professor of Homiletics,
Virginia Theological Seminary

This spring a statement was released by the House of Bishops to be distributed to all Episcopal churches. Almost 2,000 years ago a pastoral letter was released to be distributed among all the Christians of Ephesus. An immense span of time separates this Episcopal statement and that early Christian letter. The societies to which they were addressed are vastly different. Yet the statement and the letter say essentially the same thing. They proclaim a truth their recipients still struggle to understand. They tell us, "You cannot be a Christian alone."

The bishops put it this way, "If we cannot be bishops together, we cannot be bishops alone." You and I know something about the struggles in which they are engaged and the serious issues which threaten to divide them. Our common life is endangered by those same issues. Yet the bishops have chosen to reaffirm NOT conformity but community as they examine their vision, mission, relationships, and structure. In community, not conformity, they write, "If we cannot be bishops together, we cannot be bishops alone."

The author of the letter to the Ephesians put it this way: "I pray that you may have the power to comprehend, with all the saints, what is the breadth and length and height and depth, and to know the love of Christ that surpasses knowledge, so that you may be filled with all the fullness of God." You and I know something about the struggles in which they were engaged and the serious issues which threatened to divide them. Our common life is endangered by those same issues: questions of authority, leadership, discipline, and growth. We, like the Ephesians, confuse conformity with community when we proclaim the priesthood of all believers, forgetting we are fellow heirs, members of the same body, and sharers in the promises of Christ Jesus with all believers in the gospel. Again and again we stumble over the fact that no single Christian can possess the fullness of truth, struggling to understand you cannot be a Christian alone.

To say that authority, leadership, discipline, and growth are the function of a group does not deny the importance of individual ministry. "Behold, a ball team went forth to play a game of baseball. Just as the umpire was saying 'batter up,' the catcher for the home team arrived and took his place. The center fielder didn't show up at all, but later he sent his regrets. The third baseman likewise failed to come to the game, having been up late the night before. The shortstop was present, but he had left his glove at home. Two of the team's substitute fielders were away on a little weekend trip, but they were there in spirit.

"Verily, when the pitcher went into the box, he looked around for his teammates, and lo, his heart was heavy, for their places were empty. But the game was announced and the visitors were in the stands and there was nothing to do but to pitch the ball and hope for the best. But he had to serve as pitcher, first baseman, third baseman and cover shortstop and center field.

"When the absent members of the defeated team heard that their team had lost, a meeting was called and a decision was made to get a new pitcher! . . ."

I share this modern day parable with you because it demonstrates in no uncertain terms how important every member of the team is. It doesn't matter whether you've been a member of the church for fifty years or are a newcomer to the parish of fifty days; a center field apostle, or a third base prophet; a shortstop evangelist or a first base teacher; as a member of the church you are a player on a team, and you are important to the success of the whole.

Why? Because we can't accomplish anything and we have nothing to say, if we don't work together. Unity is what the statement of the bishops and the letter to the Ephesians and the good news is all about. Our mission may be one of love, wisdom, mutuality, and confidence; but this evening's lesson tells us the basis for those attributes, the reason for those goals . . . because we are one in Christ.

Our gifts, like the gifts of the Ephesians, are offered for wholeness: "the breadth, length, height and depth of the fullness of God." The author of this letter isn't talking about sameness or blandness. He certainly isn't calling us to conformity. Quite the contrary! The rich diversity he subsequently points out—apostles, prophets, evangelists, pastors, teachers—is what is wanted and needed in order that the fullness of God's grace may be manifest in our midst. To be one in Christ means each of us gives of him or herself to a community of self-givers who then have the potential for reflecting something of the infinite, unbounded richness of the goodness of God.

The importance of each unique individual, and every disparate opinion, cannot be overemphasized. Our Lord did not define the perfect church architecture, the perfect liturgy, nor the perfect person to be a member of his body. He did not design Gothic churches, designate Eucharistic Prayer I of Rite One or the King James Version of the Bible in 1611, anymore than he said there's only one kind of person who can be a member of my body.

Just the opposite. He went to the outcasts. Not just one kind of outcast, but every kind: tax collectors, sinners, harlots, mentally deranged. And he said it was to them that his ministry and the ministry of his followers belongs, because the kingdom is not whole until every facet of humanity, every aspect of opinion, every creative endeavor has been offered to the fullness of unity. What, then, might such community without conformity look like?

In the office of a parish which has the responsibility for responding to and caring for one of our senior seminarians is a poster distributed by the Episcopal ad project. The poster features a picture of Jesus with the words, "He died to take away your sins. Not your mind." It says "You don't have to stop thinking when you walk into an Episcopal Church." Rather, it invites each and every person to "come and join us in an atmosphere where faith and thought exist together in a spirit of fellowship," where individual gifts—both talents and thoughts—can be offered.

Yet how many people try to worship a brand of Christianity that professes to have all the answers and doesn't allow questions? How many equate religion with the formal logic of science rather than the rational presumptions of the substance of living? Even Aristotle knew the difference between theoretical knowledge and practical wisdom; but we continue to live as if our faith were in an idealized, geometrical argument with no bearing on or influence from practical experience.

For example, we all know that membership numbers for the Episcopal Church are down, way down; and we are not the only denomination similarly affected. It would appear that the body of Christ is not growing because only a certain type of person with certain types of gifts need apply for membership. Judging from our discomfiture with differences of opinion, lifestyle, and talents, it would appear that the apostle, prophet, evangelist, pastor, and teacher is summed up in one person who speaks with the craft of Peggy Noonan, lives without bouncing a check, and looks like Linda Carter!

We proclaim that while leadership is the function of a group, it does not require cloning. But do we really believe it? The "Outlook" section of a recent Washington Post editorialized normal human beings need no longer run for public office in the governing bodies of this nation. To be normal is not good enough. News magazines report that we as a people have become obsessed with efforts to beautify and condition our physical bodies beyond the limits of our genetic make-up. "Health," they write, "has become synonymous with overall well-being . . . a quasi-religious end in itself . . . With evangelistic fervor, Body-Building Impresario Jack La Lanne . . . declares, 'When you quit exercising, you let go. [And] the devil will get you.'"

They go on to say that today's temple is the health spa; its altar, the Nautilus machine; and its Bible, the magazine *Prevention.* "Proper eating and exercise . . . have become moral acts . . . Illness . . . is viewed not as a natural process but as the result of immoral action; and the way to salvation is a tanned, trim, taut, toned body."

Cloned conformity of leadership? Medical ethicists recognize that the attempt to perfect our bodies parallels the idea that we should be able to perfect our church, our community, our business, our world. The trouble with that idea is that anything that is perfect is not alive: It is complete, absolute, finished. And God is very *much* alive, creating, bringing forth new life every day to contribute to the full measure of his grace . . . pressed down, shaken together, and running over.

Yes, God needs, the body of Christ needs, you and I need to listen to opinions that are different from our own, to love people different from ourselves, to welcome into personal fellowship people as tall as Linda Carter; as black as Jesse Jackson; as white as George Bush; as rich as Ross Perot; as poor as the tax collectors, sinners, harlots, alcoholics in our deteriorating communities; the untanned, untrim, untaut, untoned bodies of real people to whom a unique share of grace has been given. For the kingdom will not be whole until they have entered it. The body of Christ will not be fitted together, joined so that every joint may add its own strength, until all the gifts of Christ manifested in all people are brought together in oneness.

The game of life has been announced. As individuals we can pitch and hope, but we can't cover all the bases. True oneness in Christ will not be won until every creature can assume his or her place of leadership in this community. Then, and only then, will we be whole.

So claim your authority in Christ. Minister your gifts in service to the common good. And proclaim for all the world to see, "We do not stand alone."

William Hethcock
Associate Professor of Homiletics,
School of Theology, University of the South

I

The late English Bishop John A. T. Robinson had an image he used in talking about the human psyche. His image is a way of looking at how we protect ourselves from the things going on in the world we consider dangerous. He says that most of us seem to be more concerned with strengthening our boundaries than with developing our center. We make our outer edges, our periphery, hard and brittle. Our outer edges are a fortification against new ideas or new relationships or difficulties we fear we can't bear. Our edges guard us against intrusion. At the same time, the bishop says, we have left our interior, our core, our center, relatively untended. Because of our attention to our outer boundaries, our center has been neglected. Our center is soft and vulnerable, and our strong periphery is designed to protect that helpless center from harm.

A maturing Christian, says Bishop Robinson, is called on to reverse this arrangement. It is urgent for us to strengthen our centers, to take good care of our internal self. Our centers should be strong and well attended. If we were to strengthen our centers, then the hard and brittle edges, the fortified periphery, would not be needed. We could enter bravely into risk, because we would not fear harm. New relationships and new experiences would become new possibilities for us.

II

We learn in the reading this afternoon how the Hebrew people are in exile in Babylon, where their grief over having been taken away from their sacred homeland has increased through long years lived in a foreign land. When we read between the lines, we discover that some have been faithful to God, but many have compromised their faith and taken on the religion and the customs of their captors. Faithfulness is difficult in a foreign land. To be faithful to God in a strange land is to risk pain and grief. There will be persecution and ridicule. When your center becomes weak and vulnerable, it's best to let it go and to fortify your edges so that no harm will be done.

The prophet Ezekiel addresses the faithful people in Babylon. Ezekiel reports what the very few Hebrews who have remained in Jerusalem are saying. Those remaining in Jerusalem have said, "They have gone far from the Lord." When they were taken away from the city and from the land, they were taken away from God. They cannot worship there in Babylon. They cannot be faithful to God in that strange land.

But Ezekiel has a different message from God for the faithful Hebrews in Babylon. Ezekiel's message is, "Thus says the Lord GOD: Though I removed them far away among the nations, and though I scattered them among the countries, yet I have been a sanctuary to them for a little while in the countries where they have gone." In other words, Ezekiel is bringing a message of hope to these exiled Hebrews. In spite of their fears to the contrary, God has been with them all along. And God's plan is to deliver these people, to return them to their homeland. God's message is, "I will gather you from the peoples, and assemble you out of the countries where you have been scattered, and I will give you the land of Israel."

But first, before this return to their homeland can take place, God wants to *change* these people, these Israelites. Ezekiel brings this additional message from God: "I will give them one heart, and (I will) put a new spirit within them." These followers of mine, says God, have developed among themselves *hearts of stone*. God tells them what he will do: "I will remove the heart of stone from their flesh and give them a heart of flesh." God intends to take away these hearts of stone from among the people, and God will replace them with hearts of flesh. And the reason for this is part of Ezekiel's message from God. God will do this "so that they may follow my statutes and keep my ordinances and obey them. Then they shall be my people, and I will be their God."

III

It sounds like Bishop Robinson may have been reading Ezekiel. What the Bishop says is that we are all busy protecting ourselves, building a barricade around our periphery so that what is going on in the world can't get to us. Our external fortification keeps us from knowing the truth about God's world. We dare not become vulnerable to what is happening around us lest we learn things and see things that will be too much for us. Ezekiel is bringing God's message to the Hebrews in exile. You have allowed your hearts to become hearts of stone. That won't do. No. God must accomplish a kind of surgery among the people. God's message is that God will take away those hearts of stone, and God will give to the people hearts of flesh. Only then shall they "be my people, and I will be their God."

Ezekiel makes it sound easy, doesn't he? A simple procedure. God swaps our stony heart for a heart of flesh, and that's all there is to it. It will be easy. Right? No. Wrong. God is performing this surgery in our behalf so that we may be alive and whole and mature in the world. But God isn't saying anything about our acquiring this heart of flesh being easy. In fact, this new kind of maturity is going to be difficult and painful. We need to be clear about that. Before I submit to anything like this heart of flesh business, I need to know what it's going to be like.

IV

As a priest on a multiple parish staff in Cincinnati, I was assigned seven hospitals, the same as the others, and when I learned of a parishioner in any of these hospitals, I went to visit. One of my hospitals was the Shriners' hospital for children suffering from severe burns. This was all right with me, since no one ever went there. Essentially, I had only six hospitals, or so I thought.

But the day came when our parish learned that a twelve-year-old boy had been flown into the hospital from a distant city because of burns he had received in a school accident. I drove right away to the hospital, gave the name of the patient to the receptionist, and asked if I might visit him. "Certainly," I was told, and I was shown into the preparation room.

I discovered that the preparation room is where I was to suit up in special clothing. First, I put on the loose white pants and shirt over my own clothes. Then I put on the covers for my shoes and my head. Finally, I put on my mask. Then I stepped into the burn ward ready to visit the patient.

I couldn't believe what I saw. The room was filled with burned children heavily bandaged and disfigured. Some were ambulatory, but many were in striker frames which could be turned periodically. Some were so badly burned that for months they had not been held by loving parents; they could only lie there in agony waiting for the painful ordeal of being turned once again.

I couldn't stand it. That was more suffering than I had ever seen. I turned around quickly, went back into the preparation room, took off the special protective clothing, and returned immediately to my office. Seeing what I had just seen in that ward was more than I could bear.

Then an idea came to me. I went back to the hospital and suited up again. With my eyes on the floor, I went into the ward again, and following the instructions given me by the nurse, I walked to the bed of my patient. Without looking at anyone else, I visited him briefly. Then again, without lifting my eyes, I walked out of the ward and took off the protective clothing.

That was a close call. My protective periphery almost broke down. My vulnerable center was almost damaged. But I managed to protect myself. Thank goodness for the hard edge, the defensive wall I've built around myself. Thank goodness I have a heart of stone instead of a heart of flesh. Something terrible almost happened. The terrible truth about the world almost got through to me, but I protected myself just in time.

In the early '70s, a young priest at Saint Luke's Church in Atlanta began what was probably the first soup kitchen in recent times among all those soup kitchens that have sprung up around the church since then. He saw the hungry people of his city with nowhere to go for food. He thought how great it would be if his parish could feed a free lunch to these people. He went about making all the arrangements, soliciting funds, finding sources of free food, and recruiting the volunteers to make this new endeavor work. Within no time, scores of hungry men and women were crowding into the church for a meal.

What we know is that hungry people can be a fairly disagreeable company. Some are angry, some are violent, some are emotionally unsteady, and some are desperate. The young priest began to notice that the well-meaning volunteers serving the hot soup and sandwich were uneasy and fearful, and their apprehensions were being shown in abrupt and inhospitable attitudes. He decided that this couldn't be. The priest began to insist that the volunteers look at the hungry men and women and deliver the soup and sandwich just as they would deliver the bread and wine, the body and blood of Christ, at the Eucharist. Soon the hungry were to be acknowledged as persons and cared for as well as served a meal.

Most volunteers accepted this standard, but some could not. No. Some could not look those men and women in the eye. Their apprehensions and fears were too strong. They were willing to work in food preparation and other duties behind the scenes, but they could not face the people. Their boundaries had been carefully developed to protect their vulnerable centers. Their hearts had become hardened in self-protection. They were not ready to have their hearts of stone turned into hearts of flesh. The risk was too high; the cost was too great.

V

There is a hymn we used to sing. It didn't make it into the 1982 Hymnal. It goes:

> "Are ye able," says the Master,
> "to be crucified with me?"
> "Yea," the sturdy dreamers answer,
> "To the death we follow Thee.
> Lord, we are able.
> Our spirits are thine.
> Make us, remold us, like Thee, divine."

What a silly hymn! What makes us think we are able? What makes us think we are even ready? We have gone to a good deal of trouble to build up our hard walls, these protective peripheries. We like our hearts of stone, and we don't want our hearts of stone exchanged for hearts of flesh. We would like to stay as we are, God. Your surgery is too much. We are not able. Why are you making such a difficult requirement for us to become your people? It's too much, God, and we don't like it.

VI

It seems to me that we have three choices.

We can say, no thanks, God. I appreciate the offer, but I don't want a heart of flesh. I realize, God, that this isn't the answer you want. I will just have to continue to be one of your fringe people, one of your distant friends. I'll have to make do with that kind of relationship, God, because this heart of flesh that you want to give me is too much. I can't stand it. So I have decided just to stay as I am with my protective wall in place. I'll keep my heart of stone, and serve you as best I can. I'm sure, God, that you understand.

No. For Christian men and women, this is not an acceptable alternative.

Our second choice may be to go ahead and give in to God. All right, God, have it your way. I'm mad about it, and I don't like it. It's a silly and impractical idea, but if that's the way you want it, I'll go along. I don't approve of it, and I'm not sure it will work. There must be a better way. But if you insist, do your surgery. Take away my heart of stone, and give me a heart of flesh. But understand this, it wasn't my idea, and if it doesn't work out, it's not my fault, and if things don't work out, I'll take back my stone heart.

No. For Christian women and men, this is not an acceptable alternative.

We have a third choice. This choice involves our remembering that when we submit to God's will on this, we are not alone. God is with us. And God's eagerness to make us his people is not just for God's benefit. God wants us to be his people for our own benefit.

And so the third choice—actually, the only choice we really have—it to say yes to God. We are terrified, God. We are afraid, and the idea of a heart of flesh makes no sense to us. We know that we will regret it, but our answer is yes. We know that our lives will never be the same. But trusting you, God, knowing that you will be there for us, our answer is yes. Take our stone heart, and give us a heart of flesh. We know that the pain and suffering and need of the world will crowd in upon us, but we will bear it with you help. After all, just like those Hebrews so long ago, we long to be your people, and we long for you to be our God.

J. Neil Alexander
Assistant Professor of Preaching,
The General Theological Seminary

"Keep death daily before your eyes." So declared St. Benedict centuries ago. "Keep death daily before your eyes." In Benedict's day, the rather closed-in world of the sixth century, perhaps one needed a daily reminder of one's mortality, or a word to confront the ever-present gruesomeness of human affliction and death. But no more.

I have never thought of the New York Times or CNN as particularly Benedictine institutions, but it seems clear they have heard Benedict's plea. Slip a peek at any media outlet, print or electronic, and you won't have to wait long for a story about death—impending death, unnecessary death, incomprehensible death, unrelenting death. Death so daily before our eyes that we become numb, no longer able to feel its impact, no longer able to grieve, no longer in touch with our need to grieve.

Death is out there: across the ocean—in the Middle East, or Africa, in India or Ireland; across the continent—in Los Angeles, or San Francisco, or Seattle; across town—in Crown Heights, or Howard Beach, Washington Heights, or the Bronx; across the street—in the projects on 19th street, in the AIDS ward at St. Vincent's, in the Foundling Hospital on Seventh, in the Frigidaire box on 14th and 10th. Yet death, with all of its blatancy, still comes to us like an intruder in the night—leaving us with fears and scars too deep for words.

Those of us who are clergy, together with our lay companions in ministry, spend a lot of time dealing with death. Funerals and grief work become so routine that we lull ourselves into believing that we are strong and untouched by it all. Then a death occurs that shakes our souls to the core—the death of our beloved, the death of a child, the death of a teacher, or colleague, or friend. I believed I had death under my control until one of my students died, the remembrance of whose upraised hand in the classroom is etched in my memory. And all over again, once the active stage of my grief was over, I convinced myself that if I was going to live and work in New York, I was going to have to become accustomed to being strong through the ravages of drugs, and street crime, and AIDS.

Then it happened again. And again. And again. I am certain you know what I mean.

Today's Gospel, a portion of the "Lazarus chapter" of John, is one of the most emotionally charged, passionate encounters of Jesus. Mary and Martha experience that painful sense of unknowingness that often accompanies death. Martha tries her best to keep a stiff upper lip and tells Jesus she really does believe what she's supposed to believe. Jesus tells Martha she's missed the point. Then Mary does just what you expect a human being to do in a tough spot—she shifts the blame: "Lord, if you had been here my brother would not have died."

What happens next is perhaps the most important scene for us on this day. Jesus saw Mary weeping, and those who were there to console her were also weeping. "Jesus was greatly disturbed in spirit and deeply moved." And a verse later, we are told that Jesus began to weep.

An initial reading of the passage might suggest that John is showing us a very warm, human Jesus—an empathetic rabbi and pastor willing to risk significant vulnerability for the sake of those committed to his care. But a more careful reading suggests that Jesus' emotional state—"greatly disturbed in spirit and deeply moved"—has more to do with anger and frustration than with empathy and grief. If Jesus is angry it begs the immediate question—why—at what—at whom?

This passage is difficult and the major interpreters of John's gospel do not come to a common understanding. Robert Kysar has offered these words, that speak to us with power on this particular day: "Jesus is made angry by the destructive force of death among humans. That is, he is angry at the reality of death that produces such pain and suffering as he witnesses in the sisters and their guests. The Creator is repulsed and horrified at the way in which death and suffering distort the goodness of creation and mangle the lives of humans."

And further on, "These then are human feelings of the one who is the Word made flesh and blood. But they are more. They are expressions of the agony stirred within God by human suffering."*

The passionate God of Christian faith suffers when creation suffers. In our grief or anger, in our unbelief or disbelief, in our sorrow or sadness, in our moments of joy and hope—the God of Christian faith is Emmanuel—God with us when the phone rings at midnight with news of a tragedy we could not have imagined; God with us under a tent on a windswept cemetery overcome by pain that cannot be numbed; God with us at font and table Sunday after Sunday drawing us into Risen Life!

We gather this afternoon as a seminary family to honor the memory of those of our number who have died since this day last year. We will hear their names and remember them—some close friends, classmates, others only a name, and we will be unable to keep our mind from wandering to that day—next year, or the year after, or decades in the future—when our names will be numbered among them. We should not be troubled or ashamed if we find ourselves imagining what that day will be like.

One of the most profound witnesses of Christian history is that the faithful of Christ honor with deep

*Robert Kysar, JOHN, *Augsburg Commentary on the New Testament* (Minneapolis: Augsburg, 1986), pp. 180-181.

passion the deaths of those who have gone before; but there has always been a selfish dimension of that remembering. Christians gather also to prepare—to rehearse, if you will—to anticipate our own deaths in the peace of Christ. Today is no different. We honor our brothers and sisters who have entered by death into the joy of their Lord. We anticipate the coming of that day for us all.

But let us be clear. The Christian witness to death and resurrection does not begin when a person has come to the physical end of human life and the community gathers around a lifeless corpse. The story of Jesus at the grave of Lazarus will not allow us to be tricked into believing that death has lost its sting, that the ugliness of death has been papered over. Grief and anger, despair and hopelessness, are not only human responses to death, but are also divinely felt emotions.

The witness to death and resurrection begins not at a cold and lifeless tomb, but emerges from a warm and watery womb. Eternal life begins at the font, not at the grave! "Since we have been united with Christ in a death like his, we will certainly be united with Christ in a resurrection like his" (Romans 6). Resurrection is not some cheap anesthesia that falsely numbs the symptoms of our human pain and agony. Resurrection is promise—the life-giving, invigorating promise that Christ is risen! Death no longer has control of him. Death no longer has control of us. Christ is risen. Alleluia!

Originally preached for The General Theological Seminary's memorial eucharist, on May 18, 1992, in The Chapel of the Good Shepherd.

Michael B. Curry
Rector, St. James' Church, Baltimore

There's Power in the Word

On the back of the Preaching Excellence T-shirt these words from John 1 are to be found: "In the beginning was the word." It is "meet and right" that those words should be written there. For behind all that can be said about excellence in preaching; behind the mandate and the mystery of preaching; behind the exegesis and the exposition; behind the preparation and the proclamation; behind the agony and the anamnesis; behind the hermeneutic and the headache; behind the Saturday night cryin' and the Sunday morning Kerygma, there stands the mystery, the majesty and the miracle of the Word of our God.

So for a text I would offer the following from the Gospel according to John 1:1-5, 14:

> *In the beginning was the Word, and the Word was with God, and the Word was God. He was in the beginning with God. All things came into being through him, and without him not one thing came into being. What has come into being in him was life, and the life was the light of all people. The light shines in the darkness, and the darkness did not overcome it . . . And the Word became flesh and lived among us.*

Our subject this morning: *There's Power in the Word!* There's power to summon up. There's power to save up. There's power to shake up. *There's Power in the Word!*

I

Remember, for a moment, that according to John, Jesus is the eternal Word of God incarnate in the flesh of human time. Jesus is the Word in human flesh. Jesus is the Word in human face. Jesus is the Word walking around. "And the Word became flesh and dwelt among us."

So, according to John, what Jesus did and does, the Word did and does. When Jesus healed the sick, the Word healed the sick. When Jesus raised the dead, the Word was raising the dead. When Jesus restored Bartimaeus' sight, the Word broke forth in light. When Jesus cast out the demons, the Word cast them out. John has it right. "The light shines in the darkness, and the darkness cannot overcome it." There's Power in the Word.

Just take a look at the gospel portraits of the life of Jesus and the power of the Word becomes evident. Did not Jesus say, "In this world ye shall have tribulation, but be of good cheer, I have overcome the world"?

And he did. Herod couldn't stop him, even in infancy. The devil couldn't stop him, even in temptation. The demons couldn't stop him. Lying Pharisees couldn't stop him. Wishy-washy disciples couldn't stop him. Dummy disciples couldn't stop him. Scheming priests couldn't stop him. Political Pilates couldn't stop him. The "yawning gates of death" couldn't stop him. He got up from the grave, he rose from the dead. Even the natural order of gravity couldn't stop him. He ascended into heaven. And time and history itself could not stop him. He sent the Holy Spirit and Jesus shall come again in power and great glory. There's Power in the Word.

II

In Baltimore many of us for the past year or so have been marching and holding prayer vigils and street corner revivals in areas of the city particularly afflicted with this scourge of drug dealing and violence. We've been doing this primarily in the spring, summer and fall. But last Christmas we decided to do it just before Christmas.

So we went caroling through our neighborhood, once habitable and safe, now drug-infested and dangerous. We sang carols and read the Christmas stories from the gospels. We prayed and preached and walked and witnessed.

While one would think that caroling through a neighborhood would have little affect on a drug culture, I'm here to tell you that I saw something I never expected. Oh, to be sure, the drug dealers just stopped for a moment while we were there. To be sure, we didn't clean up Baltimore's streets for good. To be sure, the streets are still unsafe and the devil is still at work.

But some of the dealers and folk addicted did stop and sing. Down the darkened alleys you could see another light beyond the light of dope-fired pipes and trash cans. For one moment there was a silent night. For one brief shining moment there did seem to be a Camelot. For one moment I thought I could see a new Jerusalem, a kingdom not marred by human hands. For one moment, just a moment, in the twinkling of an eye, I could see a promised land.

And we may not get there right away, but the kingdom's gonna come. There's gonna be a great gettin' up morning. And somehow, someday every man and woman is going to sit under their own vine and fig tree. And our children will play in the streets again safely.

There's a power in God's Word. And sometimes that power is like Jesus summoning Lazarus from the grave. "Lazarus, come forth!" And sometimes that's enough to keep you going. That Word just summons: summons hope, summons help, summons a moment of grace.

So "don't you get weary children. There's a great camp

meeting in the promised lands." There's Power in the Word.

III

In 1 Corinthians 1 St. Paul says that "The word of the cross is folly to those who are perishing, but to us who are being saved, it is the power of God."

I believe that. The Word of God can not only summon up hope, it can save a life. Not long ago I was walking through one of our local malls. I had to go to the bathroom, so I walked to one of the public facilities. As I approached the door I noticed two of my brothers standing rather ominously next to it. From my perspective they didn't look like they were up to any good, but nature was calling and I had to answer.

I went into the bathroom and did my thing. No one else was in there. As I turned to the sink to wash my hands the door opened and it was my two brothers. They just stood at the door and said nothing. I figured that I was in trouble, so I took my time washing my hands and reciting: "The Lord is my Shepherd, I shall not want . . ."

When I could stall no longer I turned to walk toward the door. They stepped forward. This was it, I figured. I said "hello" and one of them spoke. "Are you a preacher?" (I had my collar on at the time.) I answered, "yes." I knew this was it. He then said, "Well, I've been studying the Word, and it's changed my life." I'll tell you, this is one Episcopalian who shouted "Praise the Lord" for real.

The Word does change folk—maybe not like instant coffee; Jesus is no microwave Messiah, but he is the Messiah. And the Word does work on folk and change folk and renew folk and transform folk. Lives can be changed. People can be made new. Folk can be born all over again. A song writer said it this way: "It is no secret what God can do. What He did for others, He'll do for you." There's a Power in the Word.

IV

Lastly, I want to suggest that the power of the Word becomes evident when it shakes things up. You remember old Ezekiel and the valley of dry bones. You remember how Ezekiel saw that valley of dead, decaying and dried up bones. The Lord told him to preach the Word unto the bones. So Ezekiel did as he had been told.

O dry bones, hear the Word of the Lord.

And what does the record say happened? It says that there was a shaking and a rattling. A noise! And when Ezekiel summoned the wind, the Spirit came down and the bones came back to life, "an exceeding great host." There is power in the Word not only to summon up and save up, but also to shake up.

In the mid 1960s my family went to Alabama to bury my Aunt Calley. She lived in Birmingham and attended the Baptist Church where the four little girls had been killed by the Klan during the Battle for Birmingham. So the funeral was held in that great historic church.

Aunt Calley's wish was that she should be buried on the old family land near Midway, Alabama. In the South there are Midways everywhere. Midway really means midway between here and there. And this Midway was midway between Birmingham and Montgomery.

An old preacher was there to meet us. He was tall, like Ichabod Crane. He wore one of those shiny black suits, white shirt and tie. In his hand he held an old, well worn, floppy Bible. And he was the last of a vintage of old African post-ante-bellum preachers who once thundered forth in days "when hope unborn had died."

He spoke in that synthesis of African dialect, Americanized English and King James English. We kids couldn't understand one word he said. In fact, we thought he was funny. And we just laughed ourselves silly as he preached. That's what the old slave preachers used to do. They preached you through death.

We just laughed and giggled ourselves. One of my aunts came over and pinched us and sternly told us, "You don't laugh at the Word of the Lord." But we still laughed under our breath, until something happened.

The old preacher just kept preaching and preaching and preaching. It was really hard to know exactly what he was saying, but since growing up I've come to learn that the literal words aren't that important. You heard that old preaching like you hear a drum. You don't listen for the strike of the drum; you feel the beat. You get moved to the sound as the sound moves through you. It's the Spirit that is important. You don't analyze it, you feel it, you experience it. The Word is not in the consonants, it's in the cadence.

Well, that old preacher was just a-preaching. And we were all moving to the cadence and the sound of it. Then, all of a sudden he stopped. And when he stopped, we stopped. And he turned to Aunt Calley's casket and shouted: "O, dry bones, hear the Word of the Lord."

Well, like old Ezekiel, I heard a noise. I heard a rattling and a shaking. But it was not Aunt Calley's bones; it was my knees shaking and my teeth rattling. I was frightened to death. Was Aunt Calley going to get up, I wondered?

I've since come to realize that that's what those old preachers did. They looked to a God who "sits on high and looks down low." They summoned up a Spirit not born of this world, but breathed from another. And when they did that things started to shake.

They preached long ago until a Nat Turner shook off the chains of slavery in revolt. They preached until a Harriet Tubman started to shake 300 times on the Underground Railroad. They preached until the Denmark Veseys and the Sojourners started to shake. They preached until slaves in cotton fields started to shake in song:

Didn't my Lord deliver Daniel . . . so why not every man.

O freedom! O Freedom! O freedom over me. And before I'll be a slave, I'll be buried in my grave and go home to my Lord and be free.

They preached until the whole nation started to shake with the sounds of freedom . . . freedom . . . freedom. And they preached until the nation did shake in an apocalypse of judgment called the Civil War and the Emancipation Proclamation.

Our God has, "sounded forth a trumpet that shall never sound retreat. He is sifting out the hearts of folk before the judgment seat. O be swift my soul to answer Him, be jubilant my feet, our God is marching on."

There's power in the Word. Power to summon up. Power to save up. Power to shake up. Power to liberate. Power to heal. Power to raise the dead. Power to set the captives free. There's power in God's Word.

So preach it. Preach the Word in season and out. Preach it when the sun shines and preach it as the thunder rolls. Preach it when folk want to hear. And preach it when folk don't want to hear. But preach it. There's a power in the Word.

Mine eyes have seen the glory of the coming of the Lord. He is trampling out the vintage where the grapes of wrath are stored. He hath loosed the fateful lightning of His terrible swift sword. Our God is marching on. Glory, glory, hallelujah, God's truth is marching on.

There's Power in the Word.

Jane Sigloh
Rector, Emmanuel Church, Staunton, Virginia

The Wheels within the Wheels

As I looked at the living creatures, I saw a wheel on the earth beside the living creatures, one for each of the four of them. As for the appearance of the wheels and their construction; their appearance was like the gleaming of beryl; and the four had the same form, their construction being something like a wheel within a wheel. When they moved, they moved in any of the four directions without veering as they moved . . . When the living creatures rose from the earth, the wheels rose. Wherever the spirit would go, they went and the wheels rose along with them; for the spirit of the living creatures was in the wheels.

(Ezekiel 1:15-20)

Now I submit that Ezekiel's vision of God—while quite beautiful and mysterious—really isn't "user friendly." Not like Hosea's, for instance, with its cry of divine pathos: "It is I who taught Ephraim to walk; I took them up in my arms." Now there's a friendly vision.

But in Ezekiel's . . .God is so mobile . . .elusive, so utterly holy as to be almost unapproachable.

And yet I think we as preachers need to hold up Ezekiel's vision—hold it high for all the world to see. Wheel within wheel within wheel. Especially since all too often we have tried to reduce God from holy sovereign to useful patron.

Ezekiel knows we can't do that. Can't use God to validate our moral convictions and party politics. Can't trap God in a little American city—like Baltimore or Hartford or Staunton or Ames. And even if we could, something would be lost. It wouldn't be the same.

I remember once in the pulpit suggesting Sallie McFague's model of God as a friend. I was so keen on the idea; but several members of the congregation were offended. Oh, they liked the idea of being partners in creation and all that but God as friend? No way. It just wasn't the same. I had brought the eternal down to human size.

It's like . . .well, when I was a teenager, my family sent me away to a religious boarding school. And there I stayed for three long years. Instead of cheering for the boys on the football team, I chanted the Eucharist with my knees pressed to Spanish tile.

Miss Cummins was the headmistress of the school. And Miss Cummins never smiled . . .except at her cocker spaniel. In chapel she stood in academic regalia and watched to see that we had not painted our faces with rouge, that our saddle shoes were polished, and that we had memorized the hymn of the week . . .to the very last verse.

But one day that first year my mother and father came to visit. We met with Miss Cummins in the parlor—beneath the old oil portraits—and talked. Politely. I had learned the decorum of the school by then so my posture was perfect. But in the middle of all that propriety my mother called Miss Cummins "Caroline."

Now I had seen that word in print somewhere. But I am certain that no one had ever used it before that day. You see, I think Miss Cummins was BAPTIZED Miss Cummins. And when my mother called her by that other name, she looked up to see if I knew . . .how "friendly" it was. I knew.

And I also knew that Miss Cummins by any other name just was not the same. That only someone who stood tall in the sky could press me to obedience. Just the way it was only a God who was holy, elusive, and free who could press Ezekiel to obedience—not to the proprieties of boarding school, but the Word of God.

"Son of man, eat what is offered you; eat this scroll and go speak to the house of Israel. Tell them what they have done to their land, their cities. Tell them what they have done to each other. Tell them how they have been seduced by affluence. Tell them about their waste and idolatry." So Ezekiel goes. In simple obedience.

But all he had to do was eat the scroll and preach the scroll. He didn't have to write it! That's what's so liberating about the vision of a holy God—rising up on wheels into heaven. Because no matter now much we struggle to lift the shame of our people, to bring new life into OUR valley of dry bones, it is ultimately up to God. We can do our exegesis; we can find the punchlines and paradigms, but all our efforts are dwarfed in comparison to the sweep of God's grace.

That's where our hopes are really pinned. On an untamed God who can release us from inhumanity, can release us from violence that breeds violence. It's that unutterable power of holiness that makes newness possible. It's that unutterable power of holiness that makes obedience flower in a rush of gratitude.

"Oh, yes, I'll go speak to them Lord. I'll tell them all those things you say. I will. And I'll press my knees against Spanish tile to sing your praises. Just let me taste the scroll."

And what's astonishing—what's really ironic about that lofty vision of God is that only such a God can bend down and teach us to walk again. Only such a God can startle the whole world with a child—God's very self in the womb of a woman—to be born and live—right here next to us—and die in the darkness of day. Then live again. As our Lord Jesus Christ.

Whose spirit still hovers near—so near that we can feel on our face the very breath of God. So near that even in the shadows we can reach out and touch the holy within the holy.

Hope H. Adams
Rector, Trinity Church,
Hartford, Connecticut

"In those days, Mary arose and went with haste into the hill country" to greet her kinswoman, Elizabeth (Luke 1:39). Most of the iconography of this event depicts the meeting between these two women, the embrace they shared at the time of Mary's arrival. But at a small church in Turkey, a mosaic of Mary's visitation represents an earlier moment. Mary, not yet come to Elizabeth's door, is gamboling over the hills some place between Nazareth and Judah. The robes that cover Mary's womb are bathed in light, and, in what I think a charming feature of the work, Mary's feet don't even touch the ground but are kicked up, fairly flying across the hillside, in an attempt, I suppose, to show the haste of her journey.

It occurs to me that it is awfully hard for anyone to tackle the hills of the Galilee with haste, let alone a newly pregnant woman, even if she did happen to have an angelic escort. It also occurs to me that the reason for Mary's light step was the One whom she carried inside her.

What a gracious image for heavy footed preachers and for preachers who don't mind being fools for Christ's sake but don't care to be one on their own. Since, above all else, preachers are people who carry Christ to visit their kinfolk, Mary's journey is precisely the same one we make each time we climb into a pulpit. And on those days when feet stumble and words seem slow to be born, we can dare to hope that, like Mary, we will be lightened and enlivened by the One whom we are privileged to carry within.

Upon Gabriel's departure, Mary arose and went with

haste into the hill country. But it is a long way from Nazareth to Judah, and after the fifth or perhaps the tenth hill, I wonder if Mary's enthusiasm dimmed, if knots of bewilderment and doubt gripped her as she rehearsed Gabriel's message over and over. "Do not be afraid," the angel had told her, "for the Holy Spirit will come upon you." But fear is no stranger to us God-bearers, and I imagine that double doubts beset Mary as she approached Zechariah's house. What will they think? Will Elizabeth, a respected woman, the wife of a priest, understand a simple girl's story that an angel called her God's favored one? Did it really happen to me? Am I called by God to birth Messiah?

These questions are like those every preacher asks at one time or another. Am I called to give birth to the Word? Am I worthy? Do I know enough? I think preachers ask these questions because, like Mary, we find it hard to believe that God's Word will be spoken not only to us but in us and through us. The Word made known through words: through Mary's "Yes," through her greeting to Elizabeth, through the very Word made flesh, and even through the likes of us, because "Faith comes from what is heard, and what is heard comes through the preaching of Christ" (Romans 10:17). Like Mary, we are called to be God-bearers, *theotokos,* for, if preaching is anything, it is incarnating, giving flesh to, birthing the Word of God in human form. "Christ lives in me," Paul told the Galatians (2:20). Christ lives in you and Christ lives in me too.

This Good News should be troubling news as well. It certainly bothered Mary. Luke says that Gabriel's annunciation left Mary greatly troubled, and it seems that she stayed that way until Elizabeth's testimony confirmed the angel's announcement. "Blessed are you among women," Elizabeth said, and it was only then that Mary could respond with the revolutionary words, "My soul magnifies the Lord." It is I in whom God's glory is made manifest, not because of my fullness but because of my emptiness, my low estate, my poverty. Like Mary, preachers must be empty before they can be filled.

And so we come to lesson one for those who are called to preach: if prayer is neglected, preaching becomes arid. Some advice from St. Francis is posted above my desk: "The preacher must first draw from secret prayer what he will later pour out in holy sermons; he must first grow hot within before he speaks words that in themselves are cold." Or if not cold, at least so much hot air. I know. For when I have failed in prayer, I preach as a religious entertainer or, even worse, a religious expert speaking my own words and not those of Jesus Christ.

If lesson one is "Pray," lesson two is "Go." Like Mary, God-bearers can't sit still. Mary didn't sit at home musing over the angel's message, but high-tailed it to Judah to share the Good News with another unlikely mother.

It was to Elizabeth's *house* that Mary bore the word. Preachers, go with haste to bring the Word to God's people wherever they dwell. Bring the Word into their world. How tempting it often is to stay in our ecclesiastical home, comfortable in religious jargon, preaching a fascinating exegesis to a congregation who couldn't care less about the Greek for their lives don't depend on it. How tempting it also is to limit preaching to the pulpit. As a new curate, I imagined people inquiring about the intricacies of a heresy or the nature of evil. But far more frequent than the great Christian questions are the great parochial questions: Did the coffee pot get fixed? Who's in charge of the friendship breakfast? Did you know that the flower guild left the sacristy in a mess? On the other hand, I occasionally put a lab coat over my clericals and teach an undergraduate course in physiology. When students approach my desk after class, they ask not only about the nature of kidneys, but also about the nature of God. "What's the Trinity?" they ask. "Does your church have sacraments?"

"Can priests get married?" "What happened at the Reformation?" Lesson number two: Preach where there are ears to hear.

Lesson number three: When the questions get tough, remember Elizabeth's words: "Blessed is she who believed that there would be a fulfillment of what was spoken to her from the Lord" (Luke 1:45). You can relax. God has promised that it is God's word that will be fulfilled and not that of the preacher. The Holy Spirit prepared Elizabeth to hear Mary's words, and the Holy Spirit does the same for our congregations.

I once was told by a man that one of my sermons had changed his life. As my pride rose to sinful heights, I did remember to ask what pearl of wisdom had made so much difference to him. "Oh, it was when you said to be a moderate in the love of the Lord," he replied and went on to say that since his God-talk had been irritating his colleagues, he had decided to live a more Christian life and speak about it less. A *moderate* in the love of the Lord? When had I said that??? Grabbing pages from my sermon file, I found the relevant passage. "Paul counsels us to be moderate about all things but *im*moderate in the love of the Lord"—not *a* moderate but *im*moderate. Preachers, trust that God will prepare the ears of your congregations.

The Visitation was only the beginning of the gospel of Jesus Christ. In the fullness of time, the Babe would be born. The wonder of the Visitation was only a foretaste of the wonders to come, wonders even greater than the birth of children to those two unlikely mothers, one past the age of possibility, the other unprepared and unmarried. Their meeting was the beginning of Christian liturgy, a gathering of God's people to rejoice and give thanks, to praise God and share good news. And after a few months passed, the Word became flesh and dwelt among us. In the beginning, it was Mary's flesh which surrounded him.

It is our flesh that surrounds God's Word today, from

us that Christ demands rebirth into this weary world. Every preacher is daunted by this awesome task. But we can begin with the lessons of the Visitation: Pray. Go with haste and preach to the people where they dwell. Trust your God. Amen.

Joy Rogers
Associate Rector, St. Luke's Church, Evanston, Illinois

"Mortal, go to the house of Israel and speak my very words to them" (Ezekiel 3:1-17).

The word that tastes sweet upon your tongue, but the word that will churn in your guts, and course hotly through your blood.

The word that will trouble your dreams and tighten your muscles;

The word that will disturb a people's ease, no less than your own;

The word that will summon a people's memory into consciousness, even as it must haunt you with the guilty, grieving ghosts of your own soul and psyche.

This word that is now inextricable from your own flesh and blood.

God gives to Ezekiel a prophet's vocation. A vocation of proclamation and presence in the midst of an exiled people. And so my sisters and brothers is our own. For the church of our time and place and heritage is, like the house of Israel, a community of exiles. The mainline Christian traditions find themselves increasingly on the margins of a society that once defined itself in accordance with our truths, ordered itself by our values, presented itself as the product of our acts in its behalf.

No Babylonian army dragged us off to foreign soil, or destroyed our sacred sites. The exile in which we live is less graphic, more subtle, yet no less real. This culture is as replete with idols as Babylon ever was. It would wear the church as a decorative accessory, lending a quasi-divine dash of stability, respectability and piety to an increasingly destructive status-quo. The world in which we find ourselves tempts Christians to forget who we are, and teases us into being no different from everyone else.

The plight of all exiles is the same: despair, disorientation, disillusionment.

The hard-headed, stubborn-hearted folk to whom Ezekiel is sent have some reasons for their resistance. Too many prophets preached too many panaceas to a people besieged by foreign armies and domestic ills. Complacency and confusion, as much as willful disregard of Covenant, wrought unintended consequences of their own actions. A trauma that collapsed confidence in prophets yielded a crisis of faith in God. Now they are thrown back on the question of sheer survival. They are a people dispossessed of all that seemed to tell them who they are.

It is a precarious existence, life in exile. A collection of victims and misfits and scoundrels and fools who huddle on the banks of Babylonian rivers must learn anew who they are, or else forever forget whose they are. The temple, the monarchy, the promised land that once marked them as God's own, God's chosen, God's children are gone. If those were the vessels of God's presence, the vehicles for God's power, the surety for God's promises, then God is gone as well.

But there is another power and purpose at work in the world. Then, and now. Here, as there. The Word. The invisible holiness of God feeds and moves flesh and blood. The boundless energy that is God spills again into human existence and reveals itself in human speech and human action. Flesh and blood and Word. The means by which God will recreate a people. Flesh and blood and Word. The ingredients for a prophet's vocation of presence and proclamation to a people in exile.

Ezekiel's mission is an ancient one, but not a finished one. He is called to preach a people to a knowledge of themselves and to the newness of God.

He is called, not to spin tired tales of their own former glory, but to evoke the dangerous memories of a God who frees, forgives and feeds.

He is called to bring to speech the faithfulness of God to those who no longer know how to be faithful themselves.

He is called to proclaim the faithfulness of God who will work God's purposes through the likes of frail human flesh and fragile human faith. Through the likes, perhaps, of you and me.

Flesh and blood and Word. A unity completed and fulfilled in the vocation of the Crucified One to a creation too long exiled from its creator, to human beings too long alienated from each other.

Flesh and blood and Word. The ingredients still of the preacher's vocation: proclamation and presence with exiles: to a church that knows it is at risk in a world that would hold it captive to serve its own purposes; to a people who need again to remember who we are, who need to repent of our failures of faith and love, who need to mourn what has been lost; who may then rejoice at what is newly and abundantly given.

The vocation of the preacher: a dangerous witness of the hardheaded and stubborn who have a will to speak that is stronger than any refusal to listen.

The pulpit in which I most often preach is high and lifted up. A bulwark that cloaks me with an authority that is clearly more than my own; a stony womb that offers an illusion of security. But it preaches a sermon all its own before any occupant says a word.

The pulpit bears witness to the preacher's vocation. It says some dangerous things about a community that would proclaim the gospel in its speech and life. Like Paul, the pulpit announces peace and brings good news to exiles and aliens; but it is the dangerous peace and world-shattering news of the Crucified One who hangs above it.

The front of the pulpit is embellished with a series of stone figures. Hard headed and stubborn preachers, flesh and blood folk who fed on the Word and spoke it aloud to their world:

John Chrysostom, golden tongued and gifted; I rather fancied that model. But he was deposed, exiled and harassed to death by a corrupt church.

Ambrose, the unbaptized believer who was chosen bishop by acclamation of the people in Milan in the fourth century. A modest witness. He converted Augustine, excommunicated an emperor, and taught a pagan world about the salvation of God. In an era when civil authority first began to co-opt the gospel, Ambrose fiercely defended the church's independence and its vocation to sit in judgment on the empire's abuse of power.

Savonarola, 15th century Italian monk, fanatical ascetic and fiery preacher. He attracted attention with his impassioned denunciations of the immorality of the clergy and the society folk of his day.

Our own *Thomas Cranmer,* of the elegant prayers in Elizabethan prose. Savonarola was hanged, Cranmer burned, as heretics by the ecclesiastical authorities of their day.

John Wesley, whose words led to schism in this church even as he re-energized it with Reformation fervor.

And *John Henry Newman,* who left our Anglican fold for Rome, angry and despairing, yet leaving behind the words that helped restore our catholic soul.

It is no easy message on my community's pulpit. With its stories of faithful witness and dangerous fates, of story tellers who may well have been misfits and victims, even scoundrels or fools, even as we might be, even as we are called to become something more.

That pulpit preaches:

• Faithful preaching places a preacher at risk and calls others to take the same risks.

• Faithful preaching is a disruptive and divisive force even as it energizes and makes new.

• Faithful preaching can lead a preacher and people into despair and alienation even as the words restore and make whole.

• Faithful preaching is an act that judges the institution, even as it gives voice to a community's life.

For us all, the sermon on the pulpit calls a church of exiles to a discipleship empowered by the same spirit that sent a collection of victims and misfits and scoundrels and fools from an upper room to the ends of the earth. To vocations of proclamation and presence, disciples disturbing the world's peace for the sake of God's, to call a people to remember who and whose they are, and to speak a vision of what God wills us to become.

Flesh and blood and Word. It is all that it takes for God to make a prophet. Flesh and blood and Word. It is all that God needs to make a church—a people who eat that Word, in bread and wine, who taste it in the text, and touch it in our common life. Flesh and blood and Word. It is all the church needs to make a preacher.

Charles Peguy, French intellectual and writer, who died in the trenches during WWI, wrote:

It doesn't make sense.
We who are nothing, who do not last,
Who endure hardly at all.
It doesn't make sense that it is we who are ordered
to preserve and to feed
On earth,
The word which has been spoken.
The word of God.

It is our business to feed the living word from the time
in which it was spoken until the day of judgment.
In saecula saeculorum
World without end.
From generation to generation . . .
It is not enough that we should have been created.
That we should have been born,
That we should have remained faithful.
It depends upon us . . .
That the eternal should not lack the temporal
    (Strange reversal)
That the spirit should not be deprived of the car-
nal . . .
That eternity should not lack time . . .
That the spirit should not lack flesh
That the soul, so to speak, should not lack a body
That Jesus should not lack a Church,
His Church,
And it is we who must carry it through to the end,
So that God is not deprived of God's creation.

Joe G. Burnett
Rector, Trinity Church,
Hattiesburg, Mississippi

His birth was foretold by the prophet, and announced by an angel. He was named by God. He grew in wisdom and in stature, and in the favor of God and the people. Led by the Spirit into the wilderness, he emerged empowered to preach and teach a gospel of the kingdom of God, and of repentance for the forgiveness of sins.

He gathered around himself disciples, many of whom came to believe in him as the Messiah. He openly defied the religious and political authorities, and when they had had enough, they secretly arrested him and ultimately put him to a shameful death.

Some—perhaps many—claimed to have seen him risen from the dead. Despite attempts to stamp it out his movement continued; and there are those who say his followers persist to this day.

And on the Feast of the Visitation—at least in the propers for the evening office—our attention is quite unexpectedly focused on this person and his work as a model for our ministry of preaching. I am referring of course not to Jesus but to John the Baptist.

What a surprise! Here we are in this climactic period of the Great Fifty Days, and our celebration of the cruci-fied, risen, and ascended Lord is at a fever pitch. Why are we suddenly confronted with a man "out of season," a wilderness preacher, that Advent saint, John the Baptist? I must confess that as I wrestled with this Gospel lesson I was struck for the first time by the irony of this scriptural fragment which seems to me to be but a remnant—or an anticipation—of another liturgical cycle. Why John the Baptist? And why now?

My attempt to answer these questions has led me to discover things I have never noticed before, or else have taken for granted. Take for example the striking similarities between the careers of Jesus and John to which I alluded earlier. Or consider the fact of John's centrality to the opening stages of the gospel story—especially in Luke and John. In the first three chapters of Luke, for instance, Jesus and John the Baptist each receive the *undivided* attention of some sixty-five verses; they *share* the focus of an additional twenty verses. In the all-important first chapter of John's Gospel, fully one third of the verses are centered on the *Baptist's* role and ministry.

To be sure, the relationship between Jesus and John, be it their competition or their closeness, is no small feature of Jesus' early life and ministry. Indeed, though it is not indicated unequivocally in Mark or Luke, Matthew's Gospel reports that Jesus grieved deeply upon hearing of John's death, and even withdrew for a time apart (Matthew 14:13).

Of course, John's significance is such that traditional Christian theology acknowledges him as the "forerunner" to Jesus. But is there more to this than meets the eye? I believe there is.

Ever since the publication of Raymond Brown's massive and scholarly commentary on *The Birth of the Messiah,* I have been unable to read these accounts without looking for what Fr. Brown has called the "gospel in miniature," the story behind the story, the inner meaning of these events and what the authors may have been seeking to foreshadow or reveal in the way they constructed their unfolding drama.

Thus I believe the gospel writers who centered so much on John's peculiar ministry and relationship to Jesus did so in part to convey an important lesson for servants in every generation who are called to the ministry of proclamation: Those who bore witness to Jesus *then*—chief among them John the Baptist—though they possessed extraordinary gifts, nevertheless focused on Jesus.

By the same token, those of us who "go before him" now, by bearing witness to him and naming his presence in the world, must also be constant and faithful in confessing his preeminence.

How do we as preachers do this today? I can suggest three simple guidelines.

First, *we are called to recognize our limits.* Yesterday I accompanied some fellow faculty members on a sightseeing trip to the National Gallery of Art in downtown Washington, D.C. It was our good fortune to hail a cab driver who was as entertaining as he was talkative. Driving down Wisconsin Avenue, as we pondered out loud where we might go for dinner, our driver reached for his wallet, slammed it down on the dashboard, and blurted in frustration, "What with the cost of living and all that, you can just count on leaving everything you've got on the table, and maybe if you're lucky you'll get a little change!" As we came closer to the Capitol building, he shared bits of pieces of social and political commentary, including his boast of being the only cabbie who had ever bodily thrown Richard Nixon out of his taxi (!); and how, when Truman was President, "they didn't worry with protesters on the mall—they just shot 'em!"

All at once he braked hard for a light that was still green, and frantically pointed out his window at a fellow company driver across the median. "Do you see that guy over there?" he yelled at us. We nodded. "He thinks he's Jesus Christ!" The cabbie was on fire now with a report he thought we religious folk could really sink our teeth into. He continued, "That guy's been saying for twenty years that he's Jesus Christ. Two or three years ago one of his fares got so upset about it she took him to court!" We listened. He paused. "And you know what?" We listened harder. "The guy couldn't prove he was Jesus Christ, but the court couldn't prove he *wasn't,* either! So the judge called him up to the bench and told him, 'O.K., so you're Jesus Christ — now get outta here and go back to work!'"

The Evangelist John is crystal clear about the evangelist John the Baptist: "He himself was not the light, but he came to testify to the light" (John 1:8). Indeed, John the Baptist himself is portrayed as being certain of his place: "I am not the Messiah," he avers again and again (John 1:20b; 3:28); ". . . here is the Lamb of God" (John 1:33b); I am "the friend of the bridegroom" (John 3:29b); "He must increase, and I must decrease" (John 3:30).

We as preachers must be crystal clear about the same thing: we are not Jesus Christ. We, like John the Baptist, are called to a ministry of "going before," and preparing the way. We are "friends of the bridegroom," voices in the wilderness, always pointing beyond ourselves to the Holy One. And even our words do no more than name a prevenient reality.

I once heard Bishop Alex Dickson comment that "we do not carry Christ into the world as if there are places where he is not; rather, we are sent into the world to respond to him in the people and places where he is already present." Is that not the summons of our Baptismal Covenant, to "seek and serve Christ in all persons, loving your neighbor as yourself"?

Closely related to this first guideline is a second one, *that we as preachers need to resist creating dependencies on ourselves.* To the extent that I use my gifts to draw persons to myself, to make their growth in the Christian life contingent on my personality or powers, I am engaging in the dissemination of a false gospel. It is good to remember that John the Baptist steered his disciples in the direction of Jesus. The faithful bearer of the word will always seek to define the gospel, and to define herself in relation to the gospel, setting the stage for the hearers to have their own encounter with Christ. The preacher in

John's image issues a full and free invitation to maturity, not an appeal to personal attachment.

Finally, *as preachers we must realize that we cannot take responsibility for the effectiveness of our message, or for the future of the church.* We can, and should, place a high priority on disciplined preparation for this very important but often neglected ministry. We *can* seek to issue a challenge, offer a message of hope, affirm the validity of personal faith in the midst of a troubled world, and show forth the power of the gospel for individual and social transformation.

Yet in the final analysis the results of our homiletic task are not up to us. We, like John, may appear to some to be "out of season." Our invocation may intrude upon others as a disruptive wilderness voice. Nevertheless, our trust is not in the receptiveness of those to whom we are sent, nor even in the words with which we address them, but in the One who is our source and end. We bring news of the Holy One who "is able from these stones to raise up children to Abraham" (Luke 3:8b). The life and limits of the Word we proclaim are not in our hands.

So when you as preachers rise to speak a word about Jesus, always remember the words of John the Baptist: "He must increase, and I must decrease."

ADDRESSES AT THE PREACHING EXCELLENCE CONFERENCE 1992

William Willimon
Dean of the Chapel, Duke University

Preaching to the "Thinking Person's Church"

One of the most endearing qualities of Anglicans is that many Anglicans (well, *some* Anglicans) have asked me to express my opinion about their situation. The Anglican Decade of Evangelism has been good to me. I am uncertain whether or not my sermons and speeches to Episcopalians have actually produced any new Episcopal Christians, but I have certainly met lots of kind Episcopalians and have participated in some marvelous services of worship while giving advice to Episcopalians about what they ought to do about evangelism. Apparently, few of my Episcopal hosts pondered the incongruity of a United Methodist (whose denomination has been declining at the rate of about 60,000 persons per year) giving advice to Episcopalians on church growth, but I've had a good time anyway.

So now someone has asked me to give advice to Episcopalians on preaching. I am now changing roles from being an expert on Anglican evangelism to being an expert on Anglican preaching. Here goes.

One of the most homiletically damaging characteristics of contemporary Episcopalians is that they enjoy thinking of themselves as "the thinking person's church." This appears to be an aspect of the Episcopal church's conceit that it is called to be America's state church even if the United States has repeatedly told Anglicans that it doesn't want a state church.

I therefore agree with your Philip Turner when he says, "The entire history of the Episcopal Church has been establishmentarian. Even though never in fact established, we have understood ourselves to be that

127

church which is to set the spiritual and moral tone of the nation. We have, furthermore, always presupposed both a state and a society friendly to the church and we have perceived our special role to be that of affirming what is best in our society while calling its members to live up to their highest ideals" ("Sexual Ethics and the Attack on Traditional Morality," Forward Movement Publications, 1988, p. 2).

Turner is surely right about this, right also in his assessment that many of your church's leaders (the Bishop of Newark!) have as their main program "accommodation rather than distinction." Turner has in mind moral accommodation to the consumeristic culture's notions of sexuality, but I am after a different mode of the same accomidationist impulse.

Fancying itself to be the church of the establishment (the leaders, the upper classes) the Episcopal Church has often enjoyed thinking of itself as "the thinking person's church," a church for those who have a social responsibility to think. Unfortunately, in our North American context, thinking has become a deeply problematic activity. By uncritically accommodating itself to "thinking," as it is presently constituted in that segment of our culture which is high-bourgeois, our preaching has not only failed intellectually but also failed to do justice to the peculiar quality of thinking engendered by the gospel.

Modernity is the name for that project, begun in the European Enlightenment, which has as one of its goals to turn everyone into an individual. An individual, according to the definitions of modernity, is someone who thinks that he or she is answerable to no story other than the one which he or she has personally chosen. Determined not to be determined by tradition, family, tribe, community, the modern person sees thinking as a matter of severing ties with the prior claims of tradition, family, and community in order to "think for myself." Earlier, people got stories from their parents, or their church or town and then lived them as best they could. Adam Smith perceptively noticed that the modern world detached people from such parental determinism and enabled them to choose their own jobs, to become creators of their own lives. No longer was someone a blacksmith because his father was one and his name was Smith. Now we were free, free to choose; in fact, for the first time in history, writers like Adam Smith began defining freedom as choice.

We want to be people who have no story for our lives other than the story we have chosen. Yet this is also a story, and a corrupt one at that. Thanks to the likes of Kant and Adam Smith, we now know a story which tells us that it is possible to choose our stories, to live whatever story we want. In fact, our humanity is now viewed as dependent upon our ability to choose our story. This is the "heretical imperative" which Peter Berger noted in modernity. We are all now fated to choose, to make up our own lives as we go. A life without choice is considered to be no life at all, an opinion which we have not personally thought through and chosen is considered to be unworthy of free, unconditioned, human beings.

Ironically, this is also a story. We have freed ourselves from one account of wisdom, only to become enslaved to another. And one of the conceits of modernity is to convince us that we are now free of stories, tradition, communities and attachments, all the while never admitting that modernity itself is a story, a tradition (at least as old as Kant and Smith) and a very demanding, narrow story at that.

One reason why loneliness, alienation, fragmentation appear to plague modern life is that modernity has a way of making us all strangers. When my master story is that I have no story other than the one I have personally chosen, there is little to relate me to you other than that we are both living out the story that neither of us has a common story. Of course, I am not free, not half as free as I claim to be, for I have merely exchanged one master (the family, my hometown, my church) for another, namely, my own subjectivity. I must choose, I must serve the self, I must look out for and carefully nurture me. So all the while, thinking of ourselves as so free, we are really enslaved to ourselves and the victims of management by strangers. We complain about the bureaucratizing of the modern nation, but as strangers who have nothing in common, bureaucratic rules are a necessity. We have given over our freedom to faceless, nameless people who write and administer rules.

The notion that we are a "thinking person's church" plays into the hands of this tyranny of detached subjectivity. People come to church as individuals, thinking that their unformed subjectivity, in and of itself, qualifies them to think clearly about matters like God, Jesus, discipleship. We come to church reading to be confirmed in what we already know, since what we already know is, according to the canons of modernity, about all we can know. This is a peculiarly superficial way of thinking.

My friend Stanley Hauerwas often begins his classes at Duke by telling his students, "I don't want you to make up your minds about the subject matter of this course. I don't consider that you yet have minds worth making up."

By this Hauerwas means that "minds worth making up" are minds which have been formed in the skills, the habits, the practices of knowing. Because "what I think" may only be a matter of my limited experience, my meager insights, my ability to delude myself, my vested economic or social interest, "what I think" may not be very interesting.

Through our preaching we need to rescue people from their unformed and uninformed subjectivity, from taking themselves too seriously in the wrong sort of way. The gospel is not a set of interesting ideas about which we are supposed to make up our minds. The gospel is a set of practices, a complex of habits, a way of living in the world, discipleship. Because of its epistemological uniqueness, we cannot merely map the gospel on to our present experiences. The gospel is not a peculiar way of naming our experiences through certain religious expressions, the gospel means to engender, evoke experience which we would not have had before we met the gospel.

Some time ago we had a discussion at our Chapel on "The Church and Homosexuality." At the end of a two-hour discussion with a panel of Christian theologians and ethicists, a young man came up to me and introduced himself as a "baptized Episcopalian" who was offended that there were no gay people on the panel. I asked him why having a gay person on the panel would make any difference and he said because, "I have a right to define myself, to name the significance of my own experience as a gay person."

It seemed to me that, if his first designation of himself (I am a baptized Episcopalian) meant anything, it meant that he definitely was not left to "define myself." I knew that his church was quite explicit, in the service of baptism, that the church was telling him who he was, not by the conventional labels of the wider culture, labels based upon gender, class, race, or sexual orientation, but rather on the basis of the gospel. He was someone, in baptism, named, claimed, chosen, called. His name was "Christian."

Here is a very different way of knowing which is communal, traditional, sacramental, biblical. In our preaching, we need to help "thinking people" discover how unable they are to think, how unintelligible their lives are, when left to think for themselves. We really have no idea what is happening to us until we meet the gospel, until the gospel helps us to name our pathologies — pathologies which are so widespread in this culture as to make them appear normal—as bondage to be overcome rather than as fixed, closed reality simply to be accepted.

That's why the gospel never asks for mere intellectual agreement. The gospel call is for conversion, detoxification. The gospel cannot be mapped onto experiences which are already there, as if the gospel can be easily transposed onto the culture of high-bourgeois narcissism. The gospel requires an epistemological reorientation so severe that we must call it "conversion" rather than mere agreement.

Thus we can understand the waning interest in so-called Inductive Preaching which begins, not with the biblical text, but rather with the hearer's experience and seeks, through the biblical texts, to evoke or tap in to certain aspects of that experience. Assuming that modern listeners recognize no authority other than that of their own experience, the inductive preacher bows to that authority and forms the sermon exclusively on the basis of what the preacher thinks the hearer already thinks.

The epistemological convictions which lie behind inductive preaching only underwrite further the political accommodation to the status quo. Modernity told us that our problem with the gospel was that it was trapped in an ancient world of outmoded authority structures (Israel and church), unavailable experiences, and incomprehensible concepts. Historical criticism and most systematic theology which we learned assured us that we preachers had a big problem of *meaning* on our hands in attempting to communicate the gospel, therefore our only hope for being heard was to grope for some point of contact in the present lives and understandings of our hearers. Unfortunately for such homiletics, the gospel proved to be a good deal more intellectually imperialistic than modernity knew.

The gospel knew. Our problem in "understanding" the gospel is mainly in standing under the gospel. Our intellectual problem with the gospel is not one of *meaning* but really is about power. Not the limitedly intellectual problem of "How can I believe this?" but rather "In what power configurations am I presently enslaved?"

To my mind, feminist thinkers have done us preachers a great service in showing how every intellectual claim is also a political claim, a statement about power. The need to "make up my mind" is a political matter of where power is assigned in this society. Therefore the gospel cannot be transposed into existentialism, Marxism, the language of self-esteem without its being something much less than gospel. The gospel has few epistemological allies in the world, not because it is in a language so archaic as to be incomprehensible, but because the gospel seeks to reconfigure our ways of knowing, our configurations of power.

Christianity is not a description of life that everyone can understand if people just take the trouble to think about it clearly. Tillich and Niebuhr were wrong on this. The offense of the gospel is more than in the word "God," it is that God is the Trinity, it is that Jesus Christ is Lord. Calling God "Ultimate Reality" (Tillich) is a vain attempt to sidestep the political, power claim being made in biblical speech. The doctrine of original sin is not the only empirically verifiable doctrine in Christianity, self-evident to any person who knows a little Western history (Reinhold Niebuhr after Herbert Butterfield). Sin is not a mistake we make; sin is rebellion against the Trinity.

Christianity, we believe, is not a story we have chosen, something about which we have decided. It chose us. We have been embraced by this story from outside of our own limited experiences. This is an "external word" (Luther) which someone had to speak to us ("Faith comes from hearing.") for us to discover it, so in a sense, we don't discover the gospel, it discovers us. "You did not choose me, I chose you. . . ."

Inductive preaching, too much so-called narrative preaching in which I "share my story," a great deal of liberation preaching in which I am urged to "theologize from my experience of oppression," and much psychologized preaching in which I am told that the gospel is some sort of psychic solution to something which ailed me before I came to church, assumes that I am already equipped to hear and to receive the gospel just as I am. No. I must be trained to hear the gospel, to ask the right questions for which it is the answer. A lifetime to skills will be required, constant correction by my brothers and sisters in the church, confession, forgiveness, worship. In fact, I once defined Christian worship as "learning to pay attention." I stick by that definition. It is no easy thing to learn to pay more attention to God and less to myself. I therefore need to worship habitually, every Sunday, in morning and evening prayer, so distracting is my world.

I have found that part of the fun of preaching chastity on a modern university campus is that any student with a bit of sense, upon hearing chastity urged by a preacher, knows that something is afoot here which has nothing to do with his or her subjectivity, expressed needs, or what comes naturally. What a stupid idea! There is no way for me to be chaste!

Which then gives me the excellent opportunity to note how most of us modern people have nothing more important to do with our lives than sex. Unable to do anything significant for the world, we simply look after ourselves. It also gives me the opportunity to demonstrate that Christian ethical positions are incomprehensible apart from the church, that disciplined and disciplining body of believers who make me much better than I would be if left to my own devices. It enables me to commend to them two experiences much more important than chastity, experiences which enable us Christians to think clearly— baptism and eucharist.

Without this ecclesial, political, communal basis for thought, all we are left with is thinking for ourselves. The Bishop of Newark is us all over.

Luke 24 says all of this better than I. After Easter, the Jesus who came back to us is one whom we failed to recognize, even those of us who thought we had experienced a great deal of Jesus before Easter. We simply could not understand, had not the epistemological equipment, lacked the imagination to see him even when he walked beside us on the way to Emmaus.

Unfortunately for the egos of us preachers, his followers failed to understand and see him even when he "opened the scriptures" to us. Speech failed, experience faltered, so beyond the bounds of our interpretive framework was an event like Easter.

It was only when we did a very Anglican act, when we "were at table with him," as he broke the bread, that our "eyes were opened." Nothing in our cultural, racial, gender experience could have prepared us for it. "Thinking for ourselves," or "making up our own minds" could not have been the point since the Emmaus event was so far beyond our experience and minds. Is this not why Vatican II characterized Sunday worship as consisting of "two parts which, in a certain sense, go to make up the Mass, namely, the liturgy of the word and the eucharistic liturgy"? (*Const. on the Sacred Liturgy*, #56). Or, as the fourth century martyr, Felix, testified at his trial, Christians are "constituted" by the eucharist (Quoted by O.C. Edwards, Jr., p. 13, *Elements of Homiletic*, N.Y., Pueblo Publishing Co., 1982).

In the breaking of the bread, our eyes were opened, we believed, we rejoiced solely because he had come to us, come back to us, chosen us to participate in the Easter revolution. We ran all the way back to Jerusalem.

You and I can still rise to preach on Sunday because, in word and sacrament, he still comes to us, still chooses us, that by his grace, we might come to him.

Pamela P. Chinnis
President of the House of Deputies

For 28 years I was privileged to have as my rector the Rev. Edgar D. Romig at The Church of the Epiphany here in Washington. Dr. Romig, in my opinion, is one of the finest preachers in the Episcopal Church. He also taught homiletics at EDS and during his tenure at Epiphany taught seminarians from VTS who were assigned to Epiphany to do their field work. Dr. Romig was a firm believer in what we laughingly called the "trinitarian" sermon. Our reference was not to the doctrine of the Trinity but to his insistence that the sermon make three points or have three parts.

Obviously, this is not a sermon, and whether it is Dr. Romig's residual influence or coincidence I am not sure, but in talking with you this evening about important issues facing the church—as I see them—with which you will have to deal from the pulpit or in your pastorate, I want to tell you three stories. They are true stories and they have all happened to me personally within the past month. These stories point out to me areas within the church and society with which we will all have to deal in the years ahead.

On Saturday, at my church, a special convention was held to elect a suffragan bishop of the Diocese of Washington. On the ballot were four white women, one black male, one Latino male, and one white male. Had the issue been electing a woman or an ethnic minority, the decision would have been easy. But it was more complex than that. I don't mean to imply that votes were not cast on the basis of ability, because all seven of the candidates were extremely able and any one of them would have been a splendid choice, but all other things being equal we as a church are increasingly being faced with these dilemmas.

Many people feel, and rightly so, that the House of Bishops is still the most exclusive men's club in the world. Many were hoping that Barbara Harris would soon be getting some female companionship in the "junior" house of General Convention. I am also aware that there are serious theological considerations for those who are opposed to the ordination of women. I respect those persons and am aware of the painfulness for them. However, as a woman, and having been involved in the fight for the ordination of women since 1970 and being in an eight-woman support group here in the Diocese of Washington with Jane Dixon, I rejoice at her election to the episcopate.

I also know and respect and am deeply fond of the Latino and the African-American priests. There were a number of delegates to the convention who felt that if Los Angeles told us anything, it cried out that one of those two persons should be elected. The problem is that any one of them would be a good choice. How does one make a choice in a situation like that? I think as our church gets more sexually inclusive and culturally diverse, this dilemma will grow for us. How do you as preachers and pastors deal with it? I don't envy you.

Story number two. A young man I have known since childhood came to me recently in deep distress. He comes from a splendid family and received a superior education at church schools and Ivy League colleges attending one as an undergraduate and graduating from the law school of a second. He graduated Phi Beta Kappa and has had a brilliant career path. He is a member of a prestigious law firm and is on the track for partner. His integrity is without question. He is kind, good, the soul of honor, has never been involved in any untoward events and he is gay. Although he was a regular member of a church growing up he has stopped attending church now and was recently told that the review committee was having second thoughts about his being partner because the question was being asked, "Can we trust him around the clients?", although there has never been one instance where he did not behave with the utmost propriety.

When we as a church give such mixed signals to people like this young man, do we find it surprising that they drop away from church? This is going to be a major concern for you. How do you as pastors and preachers deal with it? I don't envy you.

Story number three. Recently, I was in Hawaii attending the Synod of Province VIII, the Province of the Pacific. There was to be a panel on the changing church. The three panelists, including myself, were all white. Now Province VIII is probably the most culturally diverse province in our church. The day before the panel, Bishop Steve Charleston of Alaska, who is a Choctaw, stood up and objected to three white people telling all the ethnic minorities what the future church would look like. And he was right. Shades of South Bend, I thought. We went back and forth for 24 hours until my prepared remarks for the panel looked as though they had been through North's shredder. We ended up with an expanded panel with Bishop Charleston on it and a respondents' panel with Native-American, African-American, Asian-American, Hispanic-American and youth on it. It wasn't neat and tidy but it was what the people wanted and it taught me a valuable lesson for the '94 convention. You're going to be in big trouble if you don't take into account the growing cultural and ethnic diversity of this church. That is a pearl of great price I would pass along to you as future preachers and pastors in this church.

Let me mention a few other things I believe will be challenges for you as you move out into your ministry.

In the decades following World War II there has been a renewed interest in the ministry of the laity. For too long, clergy were seen as ministers and the laity as the objects of ministry, but with the 1979 Book of Common Prayer, the ordination of women and cultural liberation movements, laity began to see their role and ministry in a new way as members of the Body of Christ. This renewed emphasis on the ministry of the laity is having a tremendous impact on traditional theological education today and, in my opinion, will make itself even more felt as we move into the 21st century. Many people pay lip service to the notion of lay ministry but it is my observation very few people really know what it means or what to do about it. Too often, when we speak about lay ministry we mean lay people doing helpful things around the church. We don't support and enable lay persons very well to do their every day jobs in the world.

The Episcopal Church, as well as other denominations, has been profoundly affected by the changes in the culture in which we exist. The Task Force on Christian Education mandated by the 1985 General Convention said in its report that we "live in a world where there is moral ambiguity, individual and institutional confusion, social isolation and pervasive alienation, where economic and social injustice persist. We are challenged to respond with a vision born out of present realities and signed and marked by our baptismal covenant.

At a pre-Lambeth Conference meeting, the Anglican Bishop of Barbados said one of the most pressing issues for Anglicans in the Caribbean was that of Anglican pluralism, as he called it. Anything goes and theologians deal with the church at a level that has little to do with the man and woman in the pew. It's been said Anglicans compromise too much. To which the answer is, "Well, yes and no." The bishop continued that too many Anglicans fail to own their own story because they don't know what it is and he added, "We fall for anything because we stand for nothing."

The cultural forces operating in the larger society have

had a tremendous impact on the church which was structured for a simpler time in our history. And just at a time when we are faced with dealing with a cultural revolution we have been consumed and sapped by internal matters—the revision of the prayer book, the ordination of women, the whole debate around issues of sexuality, the Episcopal Synod of America, decreased giving to the national church resulting in enormous cuts in staff and programs.

Coming out of the 1991 General Convention were seven groups dealing with some aspect of structural reform of the Episcopal Church. Just last week, the Presiding Bishop and I met with 20 representatives of those groups in an attempt to coordinate their work and efforts. The question for me is whether we can use the current moment to really look at the future of the institutional church or will we tinker with budgets and structures and hope that somehow we can make things right and return the Episcopal Church to its prior glory as the Republican Party at prayer. I believe the possibility is long gone to do that. We must try to discern what God is calling us to be in a culture which no longer takes us as seriously as we take ourselves. What kind of institution do we need to define and carry out our mission in a new time?

You will be functioning in a difficult but challenging time. I suspect, however, that every generation of seminarians has had to deal with that—just different challenges. The problems for the church internally and vis-a-vis culture seem overwhelming. The solutions are not readily at hand but I am heartened when I meet seminarians such as you. Take care of yourselves and I pray God's grace will sustain you and God's Spirit uphold you.

What are the trends?

1. *We have moved from a church in a self-confident society to being a church in a fearful society.* Change is crowding in on us at an ever-accelerating rate. Stop and

let me catch up. Edwin Friedman has observed that the capacity of a community to cope is in inverse proportion to the anxiety level.

2. *We have gone from a church of affluence to one with shrinking resources.* What does this mean for national church structures and for churches doing ministry on the local level?

3. *We are moving from church-wide planning to local initiative.* More money is staying on the local level. National church staff will perhaps be a half to a third their present size in a decade.

4. *We are moving away from an emphasis on "professional Christians" (clergy) to Christian professionals (laity).*

5. *We are moving from hierarchical models of church leadership to participatory models.* People want a voice in what affects them.

6. *There is less obsession on individualism and more emphasis on solidarity.* Examples: Anglican Encounter of Churches in Solidarity with Women in Brazil, and Los Angeles riots. What does this mean in terms of worship and our worshiping communities?

7. *We are moving from a single culture to a multi-cultural community of faith.* The melting pot hasn't melted. Some have suggested we are a salad bowl but, for sure, the Episcopal Church is no longer a predominantly WASP church, nor as some have suggested, the Republican Party at prayer. Can we find a way to discover how to have authentic pluralism and authentic community—a community of compassion?

8. *We have gone from a male dominated system to one which is sexually inclusive.* But how can the church more ideally and authentically model men and women in partnership in building a Christian community?

9.   *We have moved increasingly away from nuclear families to persons in non-traditional arrangements or single individuals.* How can the church have relevance to these disparate configurations?

10. *How can we arrive at a satisfactory system of decision-making in a multi-cultural church where Roberts' Rules of Order are not everyone's cup of tea?*